Conscious Neutrality

How to BE the Presence of All Is Well In the Midst of Chaos and Tension!

Break Old Patterns — Create a New Life!

TONI G. BOEHM

First Edition 2019
All Rights Reserved Copyright 2019
By Toni G. Boehm, Ph.D.

Conscious Neutrality

All rights reserved. No part of this book may be reproduced or transmitted in any form or by any means, graphic, electronic, or mechanical, including photocopying, recording, taping, or by any information storage or retrieval system, without the permission in writing from the publisher.
For more information contact:

Inner Visioning Press
430 N. Winnebago Dr.
Greenwood, MO 64034
816-304-3044

The author would like to thank Mallory Herrmann
for her editorial expertise.
Cover Image by Freepik.com: Starlite
The image is meant to depict the Unified Field of Consciousness and the waves of Possibility that surround us, at all times!

Publisher Inner Visioning Press
Published by Lightning Source
Printed in the United States of America

ISBN # 978-0-9848985-1-0

1. Body, Mind & Spirit
2. Self-help
Title: Conscious Neutrality

Dedication and Acknowledgements

This book is dedicated to the evolution of consciousness and the realization of the Divine Spirit in each person!

To Charles Fillmore, whose influence and mentoring changed my life. I never met you in the third dimension, yet your presence is and remains tangible.

To all the teachers and masters who shared my soul journey, in whatever form you showed up, I thank you.

Forever and always, to my beloved Jay.

About the Author

Toni G. Boehm, M.S.N., Ph.D., P.C.C.: Founder, Academy of Leadership Excellence (ALE): A.L.E. facilitates team and individual alchemical transformation through High-Performance leadership Development & Coaching -- "Coaching to Possibility and the Yes' of life!"

As an internationally known inspirational and dynamic speaker, author, certified organization and life coach, spiritual coach and director, nurse, and poet, Boehm reveals an expertise in coaching skills, group facilitation, and an ability to create transformational experiences. Boehm and her husband have five children and six grandchildren.

Experience:
- Unity, Ministry Skills, Peace Skills, & Conflict Resolution Consultant:
- Dean of Administration, Unity School for Religious Studies
- Vice President Education, Hospitality, & Retreats – Unity Institute
- Certified organization and individual life coach and consultant
- Academy of Coaching Excellence, Licensed Academy Trainer
- Hallmark Cards Inc., Nurse Practitioner; Interim Director of Nursing
- American Nurses Association.
- Best practice research & developer of standards for credentialing, accreditation for nursing (ANA) and for ministry leadership support (UWM)
- Professional Certified Coach (ICF)

Awards and Achievements:
- Published author of twelve books, multiple CDs, and numerous articles
- University of Missouri Woman's Council Award for Outstanding Master's Thesis Research. Research
- 2014 Volunteer of the Year Award, Unity Worldwide Ministries
- 2017 Recipient of the Charles Fillmore Award for Visionary Leadership

Table of Contents

1. Conscious Neutrality ....

    *What It Is Not!
    *What It Is!

2. The 33 Tenets of Conscious Neutrality ....

3. Everything is Energy Vibration & Frequency ....

4. 3rd, 4th, & 5th Dimensional Influences ....

5. Mysticism on the Mount & Conscious Neutrality ......

6. Alignment Practices for Dissolving 3rd Dimensional

    Fear Energy ....

    * Stimulus/Response Mechanism of Brain
    * 3 Circles and Who Am I?
    * Authentic Self, Persona, Masks, and Shadows
    * Universal Alignment Invocation as a Practice

~1~
Conscious Neutrality

*"[Enlightened is the]
one who is in unity with the Spirit ...
who in the midst of the storm,
despite the raging of humans in the chaos of material thinking,
can enter into the silence and
declare the absoluteness of his own being!"*
Ernest Holmes

BE the Presence of All Is Well!

*You cannot be enlightened and remain a victim.
It just doesn't work that way!*
TGB

*Because the sage always confronts difficulties,
he never experiences them.*
Lao Tse

It started with a dream. A dream that shared two words, *Conscious Neutrality*. At first, I had no clue as to what the words meant. Yet, every time, I thought about or spoke those two words — *Conscious Neutrality* — something energetically stirred in my soul.

Within a few hours of awakening from the dream I realized that I was dancing at the edge of mystery with a new energy, vibration, knowledge, and wisdom. I sensed it, I felt it, I knew it! I knew, intuitively, that those two little words, had a hidden wisdom message, meant just for me. And my work was to unravel the deeper meaning of their message, as I engaged in and learned from the experiences in my life that related to them.

Overtime, as I consciously surrendered into the wisdom, energy, and greater meaning of *Conscious Neutrality;* I was transformed spiritually, emotionally, physically, mentally, systemically, and dimensionally. And they opened me to a new sense of dimensional understanding and wisdom. Eventually, I observed that the idea of *Conscious Neutrality* was expanding and translating into an organized, systematic, conscious, organic, and "living" spectrum of processes of learning and "unlearning". The processes were evolving into an instructional design that supported the releasing, breaking-up, and dissolving of old patterns of perceptions and beliefs. While at the same time, consciously calling forth an interior field of harmonic resonance, and new state of conscious BE-ing. A state of BE-ing that prevails in the midst of chaos and discomfort, even at a level 10! This full spectrum of processes, the curriculum, and all my related personal experiences, became the fodder for the writing of this book!

Conscious Neutrality as a Teacher!

As the *Conscious Neutrality* meaning began to unravel, what I began to observe as a consultant working with groups in conflict, was that all the experiences of the appearance of conflict between people and groups, were actually a platform and teacher for me to learn energetically, what *Conscious Neutrality* was and what it was not!

In facilitating the various aspects of conflict management, from an energetic perspective, instead of a third-dimensional problem-solving perception, I began to notice the energetics of how chaos arises. I observed how quickly the energy of little problems and issues can escalate; how the energy of anger fractures relationships and organizations; how the energy of factions creates a negative-oriented egoic fervor; how the energy created by and living in the energy field of factions can then move at the speed of light into higher degrees of dysfunctional third-dimension-oriented behaviors and conduct; how the energy of unskilled behaviors and actions can affect relationships; and that once the energy of conflict escalates, it is not easy to recreate harmony, resonance, and alignment within a system or organization.

For even if it appears that resolution occurred from a third-dimensional perspective—someone "won" or got their way—it wasn't a real win, because invariably the undercurrents of the mounting negative energy impacted people on multiple levels of being. They are changed and an innocence is lost.

Over time, having shifted into being more sensitive to seeing life and its experiences through the lens of energy, vibration, and frequency, I began to sense the vibrational context of an experience, gathering, or event before it was evident to the group. I also became more and more aware that conflict was not about anyone being right or wrong; it was about the energy of the choices being made and how much energetic residue those choices would render. I began to observe that all choices had natural energetic outcomes and consequences. And eventually, my skills became honed enough that I could sense what the results or consequences of those choices would be at the time the choices were being made.

It became clear to me that people make choices that are often steeped in inadequate information and/or in meanings they have created about something or someone that are perceptually anchored in past experiences—not what is occurring now. Over and over, I observed that a person's attachment to their perceptual meaning-making, in addition to the third-dimensional collective and conditional need of people wanting to be right, created an overwhelming sense of feeling rightly justified to stay engaged in the conflict and battle—regardless of outcome. And often, even, regardless of options offered.

Eventually, I understood that the appearance of conflict had nothing to do with an issue, a problem, or a person—it was always about the level and dimension of energy that a person or group was choosing to participate from in the moment. Change the energy, shift the vibration, and the appearance of chaos will transform.

In times of perceived conflict, a collective choice is made how a person or group will react and that choice is made as a conscious or unconscious decision. Regardless, the decisions of energetic engagement always come down to choosing to engage from a third-dimensional, fear-based, right/wrong-oriented mindset or being willing to rise to a new level of awareness and see through a higher dimensional perspective. The understanding of a simple quote, "*If you want to know how the universe works, think in terms of energy, vibration, and frequency,*" over time began to invite me into a whole new way of asking questions.

The energetic shift into asking more empowering questions began to reveal its effect in both my personal energy field and the field surrounding me. I began to realize that conflict is not so much about what appears to be the issue, as it is about the idea that the energy in the space is out of harmonic resonance and alignment. With that in mind, it was easy to begin to envision the system (the people and the appearance) as an energetic puzzle where pieces have popped out of place—often because a new vision or picture desires to arise vibrationally.

In other words, I moved from a third-dimensional way of seeing conflict and its management into a fourth-dimensional (and higher) interpretation of the energetics involved. This shift in awareness invited both a new way of seeing the experience and understanding the types of questions that were important to ask, for energy facilitation (not to be confused with control). I began to ask empowering questions like, "What might be the energetics underpinning this appearance of dispute?"

Viewing situations (appearing as conflict) from this energetic-vibrational perspective increased my capacity to energetically sense what was occurring within in the field of the group energy. As this shift occurred in me, the way I engaged in perceived conflict situations also shifted and people felt it. More and more, tense conversations quickly began to be transformed and that alchemical transformation created a change in the group energy.

Conscious Neutrality has many subcomponents to it as a state of being. The list of higher - dimensional-awareness tenets (Chapter 2) that construct the foundation of *Conscious Neutrality*, holds the key to mastery, for the development of this state of *BE*-ing. It is not, by any means, an exhaustive list. However, when you consciously choose to establish a demonstration in mind through the rewiring of your neural patterns toward even a portion of these constructs as ways of being, you will find yourself in a more expansive state of awareness. You will discover that you have deconstructed old paradigms and ways of thinking and feeling. You will know that you are grounded in a more fourth-dimensional construct and vibration.

Conscious Neutrality holds as a foundational thesis the premise that its tenets and instructions assist in the emergence and development of higher dimensional awareness. When you BE *Conscious Neutrality* in action, you realize that you are a vibrational nucleus of energy, a field of energy. As a nucleus of energy, you are an emotional vibrational condition that everything in the unified field of consciousness (UFC) responds to due to the interconnectedness of all things in the grid.

As you are aligned in the UFC and allow a greater energy than ego-self to do Its work through you, your energy field will be luminous, radiating with the luminosity that is the essence of universal presence shining throughout your field of being. Its authority, power, and dominion are alive, aligned, and attracting through you. It is now the inspirer of the inspired action when you take it for who you BE! *By their fruits they shall be known*, and you will be seen as one having dominion and authority!

What Conscious Neutrality Is Not!

Conscious Neutrality is <u>not</u>:
- A state of pretending to be at peace and yet simmering interiorly at near boiling point.
- A contrived state of awareness in which you try to talk yourself down or out of something: *"Oh, if I stay calm, stay calm, stay calm, stay calm, things will be okay, I think!"*
- A pseudo-community in which we all pretend to be in a wonderful family relationship and yet we only tolerate each other.
- A pseudo-relationship based on the idea that if we can just keep people from saying anything too authentic about how they really feel, everything will be okay.
- Halting what is occurring in the moment by rushing to call for prayer so that any uncomfortable feelings being expressed may come to an end. After all, who can stand the discomfort?
- A state devoid of emotion, where nothing gets expressed or spoken.
- About fixing problems or issues at the level in which they occurred.

What Conscious Neutrality Is!

What is *Conscious Neutrality*? It is a natural fourth-dimensional state of being that, by its very nature, invites a more highly developed and natural response to situations – and perceived discomfort. Its development requires the capacity for spiritual mind discipline—a systematic, organized, progressive development of higher levels of awareness regarding demonstration of spiritual principle and, thus, the capacity for spiritual and emotional maturity.

Conscious Neutrality is a state of well-being and being the presence of "all is well" in any given situation. It is a state of being that is initiated as you make choices to enter fourth-dimensional awareness and begin to consciously choose to dismantle old and outdated third-dimensional structures of knowing, perceptions, beliefs, feelings, etc.

You do this dismantling until *Conscious Neutrality* becomes a consistent and established state of being. *Conscious Neutrality* becomes your norm once you have dissolved the old circuitry and rewired your neural pathways toward a new way of being and seeing. In fourth-dimensional metaphysical language, this repatterning, rewiring, and transforming of neural pathways from old habitual states of third-dimensional awareness into a higher level of fourth-dimensional understanding is known as *establishing a demonstration in mind that is both sustainable and repeatable*. Please know that even after the demonstration is made, old perceptions, thoughts, beliefs, and feelings can and will try to sneak up on you and try to catch you unaware.

Conscious Neutrality as a state of being, with the capacity to sustain new thoughts and emotions, will intentionally and consciously begin to inform your actions. These new actions will be inspired actions instead of reactions, as they are spiritually and intelligently informed, empowered, and powered by elevated emotions. Elevated emotions arise from the heart-brain and they are the higher-level feelings such as, trust, authenticity, integrity, appreciation, joy, transparency, love, peace, and more.

As a part of the quadrilogy of instruction of *Soul Mastery*, the development of *Conscious Neutrality* initiates a state of being that holds a neural repatterning process that affects the entire being: mind, body, spirit, and soul. Additionally, *Conscious Neutrality* supports conscious soul growth and the evolution into that of being a master facilitator of energy. This mastery is reflected by the consistent and practical application of spiritual principles, consciously making choices to live from elevated emotional responses, the development of higher-level values and qualities, and conscious application of all these in everyday interactions and decision-making processes.

Conscious Neutrality is a state of being neutral, but it is not a state devoid of emotion. It is the ability and capacity to hold any emotion in a neutral, mindful higher state while offering or inviting the Higher Self/Spirit to constructively express itself through the emotion. It is a state of non-attachment to outcome, while holding for an outcome that supports the highest and best for all involved.

Being in a state of *Conscious Neutrality* does not mean that you never get mad, sad, angry, or express any emotion. Instead, it means that you have evolved to a state of being where you have command of your emotions and know how to express them constructively, rather than your emotions having command over you.

In a state of *Conscious Neutrality*, as you observe an emotion rising, such as anger or sadness, you acknowledge the presence of the emotion and make a conscious choice to express it in a way that is constructive and supports keeping the energetic space open. This energetically supports you in acknowledging the emotion (not denying it) and as seeing the experience as a teacher and as having purpose for a greater good. In this consciousness, the energy in a room, a situation, or between persons has the capacity to expand, not contract. Expansive energy alchemically alters situations through conscious choice and the raising of vibration. Consciously and practically applying the four key elements (Chapter 5) will result in a demonstration in consciousness, along with a remapping and rewiring of your neural pathways.

As you are aligned and allow Source Energy to do Its work through you, you energetically dominate a space and support an alchemical shift in the energy contained within it, bringing to life new results.

Embedded Beliefs and the Claim of Dominion

"God said ... Let us make them in our image...
God blessed them... and gave
them authority and dominion over all things, and the power to subdue..."
Genesis 1: 26 – 28

Traversing the path to *Conscious Neutrality* is a journey of claiming your true dominion through transforming, dissolving, overcoming, and releasing the embedded, individual and collective, beliefs and perceptions held in place by dense, old energies; third-dimensional fear and survival-oriented energies.

This also includes all of fears "energetic relatives;" anger, anxiety, control, lust, labeling, greed, addiction, judgment, righteousness, manipulation, a need to "feel" safe, unconscious narcissistic tendencies, a negative sense of identity, environmental fears, a need to be right, a need for power, playing small, to be haughty, to be seen as powerful, acting better than, resistance, etc. It is these types of third-dimensional, dense-fear-survival-oriented, adverse ego identities, that must be brought consciously into the light of awareness and then transformed, dissolved, overcome, and/or released.

The process of consciously, claiming dominion of the I AM/GodSelf/TrueSelf/SourceEnergy through overcoming, transforming, dissolving, and/or releasing your old beliefs and perceptions, spiritually and emotionally matures you, as you agree to a conscious surrender of the adverse ego. It also, initiates a whole new sense of identity, and belief agreement, as it shifts you from an unconscious agreement and engagement with collective third-dimensional energies, into a more conscious, entry-level fourth-dimensional energy and awareness (within each dimension are multi-levels of awareness).

This new level of awareness initiates another aspect of the journey, an alchemical transformation process, which entails, over time, "deep" cellular memory cleansing, shadow exposure, and DNA restructuring. During the alchemical transformation process, the mind and body are systemically prepared and transformed on all levels of awareness—physical, mental, emotional, and spiritual—in order to sustain and maintain higher levels of frequencies. At the same time, the neural pathways of the brain are being rewired, reconfigured, and realigned to support new frequencies and information.

Initiation into higher fourth-dimensional and entry-level fifth-dimensional *Soul Mastery* awareness, initiates an unwavering claim of dominion, that sustains and maintains the vibrational frequency of the I AM/Christ/Higher awareness. This level of conscious awareness holds a steadfast knowing regarding the authority and dominion of who and what you BE as the I AM, along with a full surrender to what it "takes" to BE that I AM in action.

A fifth-dimensional surrendered state of BE-ing holds **no** vibrational alignment, nor implicit agreement, for the existence of fear energy, judgements, or attachments: not to jobs, people, control, outcomes, needing to be seen as this or that, labels as identity, old values, situations, money, being safe, persecution, power needs, anxiety, etc. These types of fear-energies cannot, and do not exist, in this dimension, for there is no vibrational alignment with, nor agreement for their existence.

Remember, the dimensional level at which you claim the dominion of the I AM, as you, creates a corollary vibrational agreement, alignment, and momentum, that creates your world. Together, they act as "creation in action." As an example, if your claim of dominion is in alignment with the third-dimensional, fear-filled, adverse ego/small self, you become subject to encountering those types of experiences that continually justify who the small self believes it is — not worthy, not enough, ugly, superior, beautiful, perfect, big shot, poor, poor me, pompous, victim, etc.

The adverse ego/small self takes great pride in gathering evidence through experiences that are in alignment with who it believes it is. The adverse ego then continually replicates these experiences in order to "feed" off the energetic evidence of those experiences. Thus, feeling right and justified, in its continued claim of fear-filled energies.

However, when your claim of dominion, as to who you BE, is the I AM/Christ Consciousness; you claim a resonance with a higher vibrational/dimensional field of awareness. In this energy field, instead of an alignment to any type of fear energy, you are claiming an alignment to the higher energies of peace, love, freedom, truth, etc., as who you BE. And thus, you will call forth a demonstration that is in vibrational alignment with the wonder, awe, and possibility that supports those energies. All done without any sense of, or need for, justification, pride, being seen, or being seen as right.

As you stop agreeing to, or affirming, the untruths of third-dimensional fear energy, you begin to perceive a new field of vibratory energy arising around you. This new field of energy is a living reality that already exists, and that operates outside of the fear agreement. Your work is to learn how-to align with this field of energy and call it into being. *Conscious Neutrality,* and fifth-dimensional awareness, claims, holds, and is a vibrational agreement to, a whole new identity, and value system. A value system that knows that all levels of dimensions, all light, all awareness, all initiations, and all information required for *Soul Mastery,* spiritual growth, New Earth consciousness development, soul evolution, etc. are available: right here, right now, in this present moment, and that it can be no other way!

Conscious Neutrality and Soul Mastery

Soul Mastery is a quadrilogy, a group of four of subjects, that forms a conscious curriculum that supports: conscious spiritual and emotional maturity; a higher dimensional awareness that translates into soul growth and evolution; and as the practical work is consciously engaged, it initiates and unfolds the development of a consciousness of mastery — BE-ing a master facilitator of energy. The *Soul Mastery* quadrilogy of dynamic, intentional, consciousness shifting instruction includes:

1. *Energy, Vibration, and Frequency*   2. *Soul Evolution.*
3. *Conscious Neutrality*   4. *Mastering Abundance.*

Soul Mastery is reflected in your life as a living reality: as you are willing to make conscious choices that support a higher-level of of decision making that invites a greater good for all involved — not just your good; as you are willing to consciously choose to live from elevated emotional responses — not lower survival emotional reactions; as you are willing to develop higher-dimensional values and qualities — forgiveness, appreciation, gratitude for little things, compassionate allowing, intentional, clear, transparent, authentic, trust — there are no conspiracies in 5th dimensional awareness; and as you are willing to consciously apply of all these, and more, in your everyday interactions and decision-making processes.

Soul Mastery, initiates a state of BE-ing that holds a neural repatterning process that affects and unifies the entire being: mind, body, spirit, and soul; where you BE a master facilitator of energy.

~2~
The 33 Tenets of Conscious Neutrality

These thirty-three (33) tenets of *Conscious Neutrality* create the foundational structure for its development as a constant and consistent state of BE-ing in consciousness, and as a tool for the development and understanding of energy facilitation and mastery.

These tenets include, but are not necessarily limited to, the following actions, qualities, values, practices, and behaviors. You BE *Conscious Neutrality* as you consciously and consistently engage the following behaviors, values, and practices:

1. BE a peacemaker — one who has tapped the inner harmonic resonance field of peace — joy, love, understanding, and …
    a. Peacemakers have tapped the field of harmonic resonance and thus, have developed the capacity to maintain the ego structure in balance and harmony, stilling their emotions on command and consciously elevate their thoughts and emotions, in the moment.
    b. Peacemakers support a higher decision-making process that ensures that all decisions support the greater good of all — not just for the good of the adverse-egoic self.
    c. Peacemakers BE the presence of "all is well"—regardless of what they are experiencing in the moment, even in the midst of discomfort at a level 10;

2. BE compassionate allowing in action!
    a. Compassionate allowing arises from being willing to BE; *meek*/humble, *poor in spirit*/egoic-will surrendered, *merciful*/forgiving, *pure in heart*/authentic, transparent, and nonattached to outcome.

3. BE aligned with Source Energy/Universal Impulse/Spirit!
    a. Yearn (*mourn*) to know and have Spirit as the living presence and energy in your life, in every moment.
    b. Consciously invite the movement of Spirit to weave Itself through all you BE and do!

4. BE spiritually and emotionally mature!

    a. Especially in your interactions with others and decision-making activities.

5. BE willing to speak authentically and with transparency.
    a. Speak &/or take action without a need for boundaries or assurance of safety.
    b. There is no need for safety in higher awareness, for trust is now your embedded vibrational awareness.
    c. BE skillful in the engagement of the art of conscious conversation and asking empowering questions.

6. BE *Conscious Neutrality* in action!
    a. Demonstrate the capacity to neutralize negativity and fear in yourself and in others, accept other views and insights, and stand for the greater good without the need to give advice.

7. BE non-attachment!
    a. Without the capacity for nonattachment, one tends to take things personally; be needy; be ego-centric; self-identify with their problems; actively court fear; make others wrong; camp in the valley of ain't it awful; collude; possess a great need to be right or to be seen as being right—which alters decision-making capacities; and more.
    b. Understand that you cannot grow spiritually without having clarity around the role non-attachment plays in support of spiritual expansion.

8. BE consistent, clear, and conscious in making choices!
    a. Take on a higher perspective and perception of reality through your choices, behaviors, and actions.

9. BE energetically sensitive.
    a. Sense and see what is and what is present in the field of energy—and what moves forward with choices that reflect high dimensional awareness. Sense what holds a conscious emphasis on the restoration of harmonic resonance and balance for the good of all.

10. BE collaborative and interdependent with all sentient beings and the environment.

11. BE and live from accountability and a solution-oriented awareness.
    a. Know: "*I am responsible and accountable for my life, needs, and actions, without any need to project on or blame another.*" You take no oaths, nor are you in allegiance to anything less than intuition/spirit guidance.

12. BE spontaneous, flexible, and willing!
    a. Be willing to be comfortable as you dance at the edge of mystery, sit in the midst of the unknown, and be in the question.
    b. Be willing to allow the questions to lead, not the answers!

13. BE and hold the capacity to see; the vision of a bigger picture, and to recognize paradox, polarity, the "both/and" in situations *vs.* seeing only black/white.

14. BE grace and ease, without the need for anger or resistance.
    a. BE present to the energy in a space without reaction, attachment, or judgment.

15. BE simplicity, without drama and complications.
    a. BE surrender, allow things to happen rather than forcing them.
    b. BE freedom, free of fear, knowing that there is 1 Presence, and 1 Power.

16. BE the dominion of I AM in expression.
    a. Claim who you BE as the I AM. Allow Its dominant vibration to support actions that are authentic, transparent, and vulnerable.
    b. BE willing to trust enough that you move forward without a guarantee of an outcome.

17. BE authentic communication, spiritual wisdom, intuitive insight, trust, authenticity, clarity, intentionality, joy, awe, wonder, peace, willing to dance at the edge of mystery — and BE them in action.
    a. BE authentic communication in action — BE clarity and authenticity in and with all the words you speak — knowing fear no longer reigns — trust now reigns supreme in every area of your life.
    b. Prior to speaking, ask three important questions; 1. Does it need to be said? 2. Does it need to said, by me? 3. Does it need to be said, now?

18. BE the conscious practice of honest self-observation, in action.
    a. Notice, observe, and then take action to shift any area where your energy does not feel pristine.
    b. All actions are free of any need to misuse power for selfish gain and are oriented toward sacred service.

19. BE a positive cultural preference!
    a. As you BE peace, there is no need to react to cultural, societal, political, or familial perceptual indoctrination.

20. BE accountable. for every action you take, or do not take!
    a. BE willing to own your story without a denial of your part in the creation of it.

21. BE understanding of, and accountable for, the impact of your energy, vibration, and frequency *on* all your interactions and experiences and *in* all interactions and experiences.
    a. BE aware of the role of energy, vibration, and frequency in the awakening, or creation, of multi-dimensional awareness.
    b. BE and hold the capacity to utilize energy, vibration, and frequency to shift/transform the consciousness in self, and/or a space, when energetic inharmony, discord, or high levels of discomfort are present.
    c. BE aware of how energy facilitation supports the dismantling of third-dimensional beliefs and perceptions. Refer to last chapter, Alignment Practices.

22. BE the energetic field of ALL IS WELL!
    a. Know that "all is well" is NOT about feeling conditionally good based on how someone else treats or perceives you.

23. BE consciously aligned with a higher awareness that knows that life is always for you.
    a. Know that life is always revealing to you, who you are and who you are not, so that you might glean wisdom through your experiences.

24. BE a contagion for higher vibrations and energy!
    a. Know that in your presence, people catch your energy like a virus and that a higher level of vibration cuts through negativity and acts as an alchemical transformer. Know you are that presence!

25. BE free of any temptation to misuse power, vomit emotionally on others, and create drama and stories for secondary gains.
    a. Forgive (give love for) and BE a state of harmonic resonance toward any perceived misdoing or wrong.

26. BE inspired action.
    a. BE intentional, focused, laser-like, inspired actions that support and hold the capacity for an outcome that is oriented to the greater good of all.
    b. Inspired actions arise from self-awareness, self-observation, and spiritual and emotional maturity—and not from fear, the need to be right, or to be seen as right.
    c. Inspired actions occur when you have integrated the skills and tools required for energetic and behavioral change.

27. BE in alignment with Spirit and higher guidance and *do not divorce* this alliance under any circumstance.
    a. *BE* a state of non-resistance and non-attachment to outcome, yet always holding for an outcome that supports the highest and best for all involved!

28. BE willing to be comfortable in the midst of discomfort, even at a 10.
    a. Having learned how to shift your awareness in stressful or uncomfortable situations, your life experiences begin to transform. This occurs as a result of being willing to make conscious choices in the moment, and by a conscious, consistent application of spiritual principles.

29. BE a space of neutrality that has command over your emotional responses in a constructive manner, as opposed to your emotions having command over you.
    a. BE a state of neutrality, but not a state devoid of emotion.
    b. BE in command of your emotions — allow Spirit to lead your every action.
    c. Consciously choose to use skilled behaviors in all events and experiences that you participate in, vs. unskilled behaviors.

30. BE wholeness, abundance, life, and truth in action.
    a. Know that as BE these in action, they become your living reality. Do this regardless of appearance.

31. BE aligned with Universal Impulse and synchro-divinity/synchro-divine events will occur like miracles!
    a. Know that synchro-divinity and synchro-divine events are the natural consequences of alignment with Universal Impulse/Source Energy/God.
    b. Engage consciously, micro-meditation embodiment practice – refer to last chapter, Alignment Practices.

32. BE a field of "right thinking" not "fight thinking."
    a. Stand for justice through conscious consciousness and having the capacity for alchemical transformation through your presence — BE an oasis of strength.

33. BE! This list is not exhaustive!

Alchemical Transformation & the Witnessing of Another

If the tenets hold a glimmer of truth, then how do you begin to practically apply them, and the other instructions, in your life? How do you support change in yourself, and in the world?

Although many examples are given throughout the book, one simple way, which requires spiritual discipline of thoughts and feelings, is the process known as alchemical transformation witnessing of another. Alchemical transformation witnessing is the conscious witnessing of another from a higher level of awareness instead of witnessing who they appear to be.

How does alchemical transformation witnessing work or happen? Let's start with how it doesn't happen. It doesn't happen when you see or perceive an individual (or a group) to be who and what you think they have always been: she is bossy, he is overbearing, she is so weak, she is controlling, he is greedy, or they are evil. When you do that, all you are doing is reaffirming what you have thought or believed to be true in your thinking as a past perception about them.

Knowing and thinking are the not the same thing. When you *know* someone as truth, you are investing in thoughts that arise from a higher dimension of awareness—the level of truth.

When you think about someone from your past perceptions, you are investing in your own perception of what you think they are, which ultimately means nothing.

Remember, alchemical transformation is about the changing of a substance from one form to another while the original substance never changes. The patterns of form shift (moisture → water → ice) and the substance appears different or changed, but the underlying energy or substance is the same. When you witness someone in truth, as TRUTH, you are shifting the alchemical structure of how you see them—as you KNOW them in TRUTH, and you see them anew. We are all the same at the level of structure.

When you look at someone and witness them as a mother, father, brother, sister, enemy, rival, the one who did this or that, you are witnessing them based on a past perception of knowing in time, based on form in personality.

When you make a claim for another—*I behold the Christ, Buddha, High Truth in you*—you are making the claim that you know who they are in higher dimensional awareness, in truth. I see you outside your physical form. I see you at the primordial level of structure. I see you as pure being.

All this simply means that you witness them outside of a pre-prescribed structure of perception that you have assigned to them based on previous experiences and even previous learnings given to you by others. Predefined structures of knowing—such as the "always late one," the "angry one," the "bossy one," the "one who can't be counted on," the "immature one," the "uncaring one," the "selfish one," and so on—color your view of truth and reality.

In a moment of conscious allowing, of BE-ing receptive to a higher truth, you align them to what they truly are. As you witness them differently in consciousness, you begin to see them differently. Understand the difference here! *I behold the Christ in you* doesn't mean *I think I know this,* or *I think I know who you are.* It is not a platitude you created. Until you understand the magnitude of this and have a clear realization of the deep meaning of *I behold the Christ in you* and *I KNOW who you are in Truth*, you are just playing a game of platitudes. Who you think anyone is – is always a false identification based on perceptions. This is not about looking at a person who is not well and seeing them well because that is what you wish for them. NO! This is bigger than that!

This works whether it is about witnessing a person differently, seeing wholeness, seeing abundance, or any other spiritual principle as a *living* truth. This is a high-level awareness of the capacity to recognize the divine and inherent worth AS the divine. By claiming and holding that awareness of TRUTH, an alchemical transformation takes place in the energy field.

~3~
Everything is Energy, Vibration, and Frequency

> *If you want to know how the Universe works*
> *think in terms of energy, vibration, and frequency.*
> Nicola Tesla

Which came first? The idea of *Conscious Neutrality*? Or, the understanding of the role of energy, vibration, and frequency? I cannot say. Each is, now, so intertwined within my BE-ing, that they are one unit, working in unity, to create and support the experiences of my life.

Transforming Energy!

> *The mind and body ... have power to transform energy*
> *From one plane of consciousness*
> *[3rd D., 4th D., 5th D....] to another.*
> *This is the power and dominion implanted from the beginning...*
> *And the climax is set forth in the resurrection and ascension.*
> Charles Fillmore[1]

Nicola Tesla said, "*If you want to know how the universe works, think in terms of energy, vibration, and frequency.*" Discovering this statement serendipitously and dramatically shaped a new direction for my spiritual evolution and education.

As I tapped into a deeper awareness of the hidden wisdom, life-shifting energies, and palpable higher-dimensional vibrations concealed within the context of that simple phrase, my life dramatically changed. My perspective on how to interact and participate with people, experiences, life, the universe, multidimensional awareness, and the creation of a "living" reality totally and completely shifted. In many ways it was an unlearning process. The unwinding of the mystery and secrets of that quote

---

[1] Charles Fillmore, *Revealing Word*, 151.

eventually evolved a new level of vibration and frequency within my being and supported a greater awareness and understanding of what *Conscious Neutrality* means.

I Am a Vibrational Being, Living in a Vibrational Universe

In the realization that everything is energy, vibration, and frequency, I began to see with great clarity that I lived in a vibrational universe and that I was a vibrational being having a spiritual-vibrational experience in a human form. What I held as a vibration—in the form of thought, feelings, and emotions—mattered to my soul growth and awareness. It mattered to the creation and development of both my spiritual experience and my experience of physical reality.

I realized that energy and vibration doesn't lie: it reveals! But only to those who have *eyes to see.* Saying that energy doesn't lie means that you can't say one thing and feel or act the opposite of what you just said. The true energy of the situation will be revealed.

If you say, "I am Love in expression," and then immediately get angry or feel anger toward someone, that creates a space of incoherent energy. And it will be felt. Or if two people are fighting and they assure someone who has just walked in to the room that everything is just fine, regardless of the words, the true energy in the room will be felt by someone who is sensitive to vibrations.

This is not about right or wrong—it is about creating alignment with what you say and feel and with who you BE. If you affirm, "I am abundance in action," then continually bemoan how in debt you are, this creates a resistance in the energetic field of your being and words against that which you are working to demonstrate. From an energetic perspective, that energy of resistance will set up a subtle vibrational signal that is incoherent and will vibrationally thwart the attraction of higher ideas and possibilities to you. And those with ears to hear and eyes to see will sense the resistant energy in your field regardless of the happy words or feelings you speak and share.

Someone will take notice of the energetic incoherence between your energy field and your words and actions. This is not about a one-time event—this is about showing up consistently in an incoherent way and yet believing that you are coherent. If you are "lucky" or "blessed," someone will point out the incoherency to you. At first, you probably won't like it. But as you spiritually awaken, you will appreciate the feedback and begin to see it more clearly for yourself. This act of seeing for yourself or "looking" is known from a spiritual context as honest self-observation and being your own witness.

Honest self-observation is a spiritual milestone because spiritual growth can only truly begin when you start to practice self-observation. It means honestly observing, without qualification or excuses, all your thoughts, feelings, behaviors, and actions. *If you can see it, you don't have to be it!* You don't have to be it if you can see it, for in that moment you can make a new choice as to what you energetically want to create and demonstrate in your life experiences. And that is where real spiritual and emotional growth and maturity occurs.

Over the decades, I have come to realize that it is not enough to see your own incoherent, unskilled behaviors or actions and then apologize for them happening. Lots of people see their incoherent (unruly, unkind, bad, negative) behaviors and apologize repeatedly. "I promise I will never hit you again." Or they continually answer their phones and text when they have been asked to shut them off or put them on vibrate. They apologize, say they are sorry for their actions, but they do not take any action to change their behaviors.

It is only when you honestly observe the incoherence in your thoughts, feelings, or actions—and then make a conscious choice to take an action to support a shift of your energy through your behaviors and actions—that a true change can occur. It is only when you choose to shift into energetic coherence that you begin to experience what is known as *alchemical transformation*.

Alchemical Transformation

Alchemical transformation! It occurs around us and within us, but few know what it is or what it means. Alchemy is simply the transformation of a substance, changing it from one form to another. Alchemy occurs when the energy level or frequency that a substance is vibrating at changes—think ice to water or water to steam. Alchemical transformation is not woo-woo; it is a spiritual process.

This transformation occurs in you when you experience a sudden, and often unexpected, internal frequency shift that changes the dynamics of who you BE—and/or the dynamics of who you BE shifts the energy field, in which you are engaged with others.

It has been said, *"Everything is energy and that's all there is to it. Match the frequency of the reality you want, and you cannot help but get that reality. It can be no other way . . ."* Your consciousness changes when the energy and vibration you carry shifts! And that shift invites you into seeing from higher dimensions of awareness.

As you begin to view things from an energetic, vibrational, and frequency perspective, you start to see or sense experiences, people, and situations in a new way. You sense experiences from the context of the questions: *What might energetically be happening here? What might be occurring within this energetic field?* Which is different from, *Something is wrong, who is to blame?*

Empowering/Quantum Causing Effect Questions

Shifting to this type of question invites a subtle shift in perspective and meaning in the moment. I call these types of questions *Empowering Questions and Quantum Causing-Effect Questions*. These types of questions have the capacity to shift perception and move your mind-focus from a third-dimensional context—*What just happened here? Who is right or wrong, who is to blame, or how can I be right in this situation?* —to perceiving the situation from a sense of non-attachment, non-resistance, and not taking anything personally in the moment.

An empowering/quantum causing-effect question has the capacity to open the energetic field and invite a sense (experience) of perceiving things differently, simply because an empowering question allows a new wisdom to arise that comes from a higher perspective. That perspective is both spiritual and scientific in orientation. It is scientific in the sense that it has the capacity to stop the amygdala's fight-or-flight response and to kickstart a response from the executive centers in your frontal lobe. It is spiritual in the sense that shifting to the executive response center opens the field to a higher wisdom answer, for resistance has been decreased or eliminated.

Empowering/Quantum Causing-Effect Questions include:

> *What is important here?*
> *What might be important here?*
> *What meaning am I giving to this?*
> *What is energetically occurring here?*
> *What might be a contribution here?*
> *How might I BE a contribution here?*
> *What would a person who is ___ (abundant, centered, excited about life, etc.) be feeling right now?*

Remember, everything is energy, vibration, and frequency. You live in a vibrational universe and you are a vibrational being having a spiritual-vibrational experience of evolution in a human form. Know that soul evolution is as much about your physical form (what you do and the actions you take) as it is about your non-physical form (the energy and vibration you take your actions from). It is said that the dash between birth and death (19_ – 20_) is a short span, so use it wisely!

Things are manifested in your life in alignment with the vibrational energy (thought and feeling) that you hold regarding who you claim to BE/I AM. *I am worthy to receive, or not!* It is your choice, for the law works. Right use or reverse use, the law works!

The ability to read energy is neither strange nor unconventional, nor it is something special that only a few people can attain. Reading energy is an inherent yet latent talent and the more we awaken to higher levels of awareness, the more awakened that talent becomes. Along with other talents, too. Have you ever thought of someone and the phone rings, and you pick it up only to find out it's them? That is *telepathy* at work in you!

These are natural responses of BE-ing when you are in energetic alignment and connection to Universal Source Energy. The more you are willing to dissolve and release third-dimensional baggage and to release resistance, the less energetic static there is to block or interfere with higher dimensional messages and intuitive hints that are always being broadcasted. Remember, you stand in the midst of all things now! Higher potentials and possibilities are available to you now!

As you consciously remove the energetic blocks, you will free up space for new ideas to flow through you. When you are an open and clear channel, energy flows. Children often hold this energy until they are impacted by the realities of life. When I was about ten years old, my friend and I decided to go see her grandma, which required a long walk through the woods. I remember that even at that young age, I loved the quiet of the woods and the sense of being a part of nature.

About a quarter of a mile from her grandma's house, we saw her grandma's neighbor. We were very surprised because she had been very ill. She was tending to her beloved garden and she waved when she saw us. We waved back, and then she turned and walked into the woods. My friend and I looked at each other and thought that it was strange that she walked into woods. At her grandma's, we mentioned that we saw her neighbor and how good she looked. Her grandma looked at us strangely and said, "Girls, you couldn't have seen her. She died this morning." Can I explain what happened? No! Are we certain we both saw her? Yes!

Everything is energy, vibration, and frequency. It is how the universe is set up and how it works. Stated very simply, from a metaphysical perspective, energy is the dynamic substance that underlies and ultimately connects all things. All energy is set into motion through vibration. Vibration is a rate of motion and that motion creates a momentum, or movement, of energy. Vibrational momentum aligns with and emits a frequency. Think of vibrational momentum as a radio station that is tuned to a specific frequency. You can tune into various stations that hold different frequencies by turning the dial.

The level of frequency determines the amount of knowledge, light, and wisdom contained within the vibration and its frequency range. The frequency range determines the dimensional level at which the energy is vibrating. And energy doesn't lie.

Know that the shifting dimensional perception occurs through consciousness. How you perceive these dimensions will determine what information (light/wisdom/knowledge) you allow to come into you and through you. Remember, it is the vibrational intention and vibrational atmosphere that you allow to be present through your consciousness that underpins what you do and that makes the difference in working with energy and vibration.

You cannot say, "I know I vibrate at a fourth-dimensional level," and then have all your words, emotions, and actions be third-dimensional lower survival-oriented expressions. People will notice the incoherence. This means that you cannot say you stand for love and act out hateful actions or walk around with a chip on your shoulder, reacting to every little thing that is said that you don't agree with. People will feel the incoherence that is emitted through your energy field.

Your energy field is an energetic field that surrounds your body and that is palpable to those who sense energy. It was often said of the Master Teacher Jesus, ". . . and he read their hearts." Which, in today's language, means that he read their field of energy. Then he knew what to do in any given situation—and often he just left.

Bridging the Dimensions

> *You cannot solve a problem*
> *on the same level of consciousness that created it.*
> Albert Einstein

Charles Fillmore shared nearly a hundred years ago that "Unity [metaphysical teachings] is a bridge between the third and fifth dimension." Meaning, it is a fourth-dimensional teaching calling forth higher dimensional awareness. I found this to be an extremely interesting concept at the time, and yet I did not quite understand the impact it would have on my life.

Years later, I discovered that both Mr. Fillmore and Ernest Holmes (founder of Centers for Spiritual Living) shared in their writings the assertion that dimensions are not locations or places, but levels of consciousness that vibrate at different rates.

This statement supported an unlocking of mind-memories that had previously been shut away, under lock and key, in the deep recesses of my consciousness. And an expansiveness of consciousness began to take place. Mystical visions and synchro-divine events occurred (those unexpected moments when the Universal Intelligence aligns people, situations, and conditions and the seemingly miraculous occurs and changes you). Simultaneous realities appeared, revealing the different outcomes available based on my choices, as did a desire for transparency-authenticity in all my undertakings, telepathy, and other miracles beyond my normal comprehension. All of this started to be normal.

I began to explore new dimensions of understanding regarding the life of the Master Teacher Jesus. I discovered that whether I believed Jesus lived or did not live was of no consequence. What was important was that I saw the spiritual legacy that was left through the mystical writings and stories regarding his life experiences and that there was profound teaching hidden within them. As my eyes and heart opened, I began to see that this legacy was a blueprint or a template for *Soul Evolution, Soul Mastery,* and the journey into higher realms and dimensions of awareness—the Kingdom of Heavens.

A Universal Multidimensional Matrix

Dimensions are not places or locations
but levels of consciousness, each vibrating at different rates.
Charles Fillmore & Ernest Holmes

"*Unity [metaphysical teaching] is the bridge between third and fifth dimensions.*" The following chart, **Example A**, depicts that dynamic movement of energy, vibration, and frequency across dimensions. Each dimension is held in place by the energy, light, information, and knowledge that match the underlying energy, vibration, and frequencies. These work together to create and hold the foundational thought and belief constructs held within the dimensions—third, fourth, fifth, etc. (Refer to **Example B** for a list of those constructs and beliefs.)

Example A shows, in a simple format per Fillmore, where the metaphysical movement sits within the dimensions as a construct. Metaphysics and its inherent teachings are said to be a bridge that has the capacity to lift you out of third-dimensional thinking and move you into the multiple levels and portals held within fourth-dimensional awareness. As a person progresses (like the Master Teachers Jesus and Buddha), they move into higher and higher expressions of fourth-dimensional and fifth-dimensional energy fields.

Example A: A Universal Multidimensional Matrix

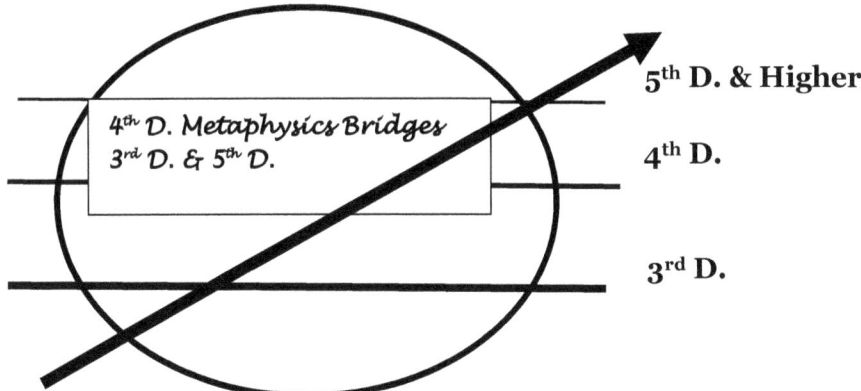

Each dimension is an energy field and frequency range. (Matrix: an environment in which something develops.)

The higher the dimension, the finer the frequency and energy that is in that dimension (as represented by the lightening of the representative dimensional lines). One who tunes into that frequency field or range sees from a state of awareness that matches the information and knowledge that the frequency range holds. Alignment with higher dimensional awareness speeds up energy and has the capacity to manifest things more quickly. At higher frequencies, energy moves faster.

As each dimension holds different frequencies, each requires different capacities to sustain the information, knowledge, and wisdom contained within its range. The work involved in the creation of mastery in consciousness over the elements of the third dimension is not about focusing on how to solve the problems of your life. The work is to master learning how to shift the energy, vibration, and frequency from which you view and participate with life. Once you demonstrate or master a higher level of understanding in your consciousness, it becomes a part of your energy field or range, and it lives in your cellular memories.

Thus, it acts vibrationally as a point of attraction for the working of the law on your behalf. The law then goes forth into the greater field to match up the cooperative components required for the manifestation of your request, thereby matching up and drawing to you all the components (people, situations, conditions, etc.) that are in alignment with your vibrational signal.

The spiritual path, the spiritual journey, the journey of awakening, the path to ascension—whatever name you choose to use—is a path of rising frequencies. It is a path of ascension in consciousness and awareness. It is about attaining new levels of frequency, entering new dimensions of understanding, and opening new portals of information.

However, this energetic rising in consciousness requires that we master each level of frequency to sustain it and hold it steady in our mind. Once a new level of awareness is mastered, it then works effortlessly in our life. It is not unusual to have what appears to be an instantaneous awakening moment. Although it happens in an instant, know that there have been years of conscious and unconscious preparation behind it. If this happens to you as an individual, then what does it mean for the collective whole as a species?

As a species, there is a collective awakening occurring. People are shifting into new levels of lower fourth-dimensional awareness. Many are observing that things are speeding up and manifesting faster, and they are sensing changes within them. What does an energetic movement into higher dimensions feel like? Here a few of the signs that people are sharing.

Do you sense that you are strangers in a strange land? Do you find things that have always worked are no longer working? Do you notice that you are no longer relating to people you have always related to? Or do things you used to enjoy no longer have the verve they once did? Do you often find that rather than wanting to run around thither and yon, you find yourself wanting to stay home and BE? Have you noticed or had a sense that your energy is shifting?

Is your body having strange sensations, like being tired even when you know you are not? Do you feel scattered when you thought you were clear? Do thoughts disappear out of your mind and, like whoosh, they are gone? Do you feel anxious when you know you aren't? Do you feel sad when you know you aren't? Do not despair.

You are going through some energetic dimensional shifts. Be appreciative that you are sensitive enough to be aware that something is going on.

Do you notice that when you look at a clock or a group of numbers that the numbers are sequential? 5:55, 1:11, 3:33! These are messages affirming your connection to Source Energy. The following is my personal interpretation of what it means when sequential numbers appear:

1:11 = angels are nearby
2:22 = good is coming
3:33 = masters and guides are nearby
4:44 = more about angels
5:55 = change is in the wind
6:66 = about balance and observing
7:77 = miracles and success are coming
8:88 = progress, moving forward
9:99 = you are complete on some level
10:10 = one with Source-energy is increasing exponentially
11:11 = mastery
12:12 = mastery and spiritual completion

If you are experiencing these signs, know that you are open to or opening to higher dimensions of awareness. Your work is to consciously chose in each moment to keep your vibration focused on elevated thoughts/feelings. Do not lower your energy by engaging in the petty exchanges of everyday life experiences.

Honestly, observe when your desire is to be seen as right or special and remain above the fray of chaotic discord that tries to seduce you into its clutches. Know that you don't need anyone to have your back. You need no protection except the power of the open heart, a power that arises from your connection with universal higher-heart intelligence, that cosmic connection that aligns you with Universal Intelligence and the unified field of consciousness and higher possibility.

Universal Alignment Invocation

The swift powerful activity of Universal Intelligence
now releases from me
all thoughts, beliefs, behaviors, ideas, and energies
that <u>are not</u> in vibrational alignment with
the universal principles of truth.

The swift powerful activity of Universal Intelligence
now attracts to me
all persons, thoughts, beliefs, behaviors, ideas, and energies
that <u>are</u> in vibrational alignment with the
universal principles of truth and the
highest possibilities in the unified field of consciousness.

~4~
Third-, Fourth-, & Fifth-Dimensional Frequency Influences[2]

*Learn how to see how everything
connects to everything else.*
Leonardo Da Vinci

The Universe Is an Ever-Expanding YES!

Charles Fillmore said that *"life is an ever-progressive, ever-expanding, ever-evolving, upward spiral of conscious evolution."* Astrologers and other metaphysical teachers are saying that since the eclipse of 2012, there are multiple types of evolutionary shifts going on. Earth shifts, body shifts, DNA shifts, climate shifts, seismic shifts, dimensional shifts, perceptional shifts, brain-wiring shifts, and sleep-state shifts, to name a few. These shifts are occurring more and more rapidly.

Fillmore also said that the subconscious mind was designed to take imprints from Source Energy/Spirit/God, but because of freewill you have chosen to take direction from third-dimensional experiences and awareness. And that choice has created the discord and inharmonic resonance that you and many others are experiencing. It is time to "lift up your eyes and see fields ripe for harvest."

It is time to see that being open to new levels of multidimensional experiences and thinking will move you in new directions that will evolve you. It appears that the upward spiral of evolution is occurring now. The changes being experienced are shifts into higher dimensional awareness, and they portend the new information that is being vibrationally imprinted regarding who we BE. These shifts are occurring globally, collectively, and individually. They are inviting you to let go and to learn how to dance at the edge of mystery. However, even though many are awakening, there are still

---

[2] Boehm, *Mastering Abundance*, Ch. 10, 11 ,12.

many who do not have the tools to recognize what is happening nor the skills to manage it.

As recently as fifteen or twenty years ago, if someone would have spoken to me about dimensional shifts and multidimensional aspects of being, I might have laughed and said, "Oh, a New Age hippie expounds again." Even though I had multiple mystical experiences over and over, I either denied them or often downplayed them. It took years for me to begin to own my sense of BE-ing and to realize the glory and grace in the I AM that I AM.

After having my own experiences with multidimensional shifting, I am now an empirical knower. Aspects of my being have been opened, gifts have been awakened, imprints have been downloaded, and mysteries have been unlocked. Once the proverbial cat is out of the bag, it is difficult to get it back in—and frankly, I do not want to go back.

This is an evolutionary time. You are in an evolutionary cycle, and this cycle will not allow status quo to remain. Therefore, the work is not about looking for what is right or wrong or who is right or wrong. It is about conscious evolution. How are the experiences in front of me serving as my teachers? How is the vibration I am currently experiencing serving my soul growth? Does this vibration, feeling, or emotion serve greater alignment?

You are energy, an energetic being, an electromagnetic field of walking-talking vibrational energy. The electromagnetic field around you is specific to you and contains vibrationally encoded information and data and, whether you see it or not, it is there radiating around and from you. As a field of energy, you are broadcasting signals all the time.

As an energy field, you attract what you place your attention and intention on, and this makes all the difference when it comes to being and living as one who attracts greater good, abundance, and love—or not. The work is to learn to manage your vibration and your field of energy—and to be more sensitive to the presence of resistance when it shows up in your life experiences. Resistance slows energy movement.

When you say you want to grow and change and then do things that are out of alignment with who you say you are or what you want to experience, you will feel the kickback of the two energies colliding (the energies of wanting to flow with things yet being in resistance to them). Be sensitive to it. Do not ignore it. Sense it and be interested in the possibility that you might be out of alignment.

The learning that comes as you traverse the landscapes of new realities is that you cannot take your third-dimensional baggage with you. You must be willing to mature and release the limitations of your will/ego to move forward. To continue the journey into higher dimensional awareness, you must be conscious, awake, aware, and cognizant of how you are showing up in each moment. To do that requires that you live with a sense of clarity, intentionality, coherency, transparency, authenticity, and accountability in everything you do.

Remember, all dimensions exist right here, right now! That is why there is nothing to get, only layers of muck to peel away. That unpeeling then reveals a new level of light, understanding, and awareness—which shifts how you see your current reality. This is not about comparing right or wrong. There is no right or wrong; the reality you choose to live from is simply where you reside until you don't.

The work, as you traverse the spiritual journey, is to awaken you to new dimensions of reality. Interestingly, most people do not choose to awake until they are in the midst of some great emotional drama. This can be a level of resistance with no apparent solution at hand, a traumatic situation, a dark night of the soul, a dark night of the ego, or what have you. Each of these experiences has the inherent capacity to call forth a yearning to open the heart to a new level of awareness for life and its experiences.

The following is a descriptive overview of third-, fourth-, and fifth-dimensional constructs, influences, behaviors, and actions. Notice and observe the differences between the dimensions and honestly consider what shifts might be required for you to engage a new level of awareness!

Overview of Body, Light, and Dimensions

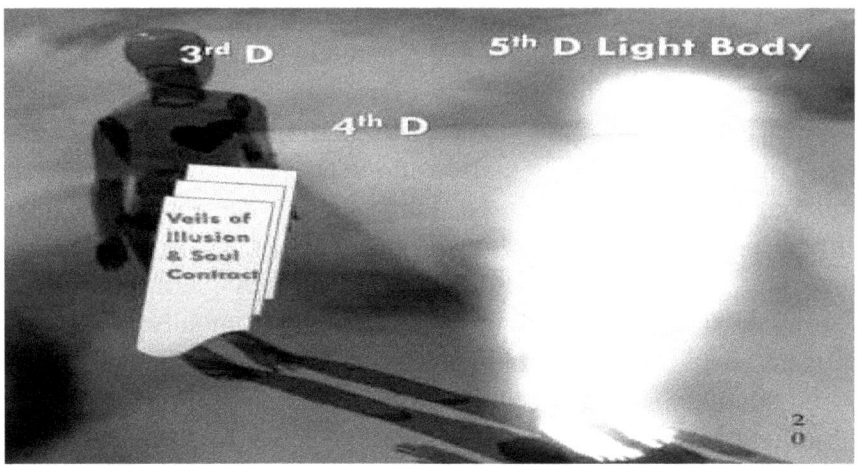

Third Dimension (Realm of Appearance): Requires the transmutation and dissolving of the dense energy of perceived separation and the embedded perceptual beliefs of humankind and family dynamics, which includes all attachment to "My Personal Story." You are here to pierce the veils of illusion and to learn how to ascend into higher dimensions of awareness & BE a master facilitator of energy.

Fourth Dimension (Activation and Integration through Intention): Activates inner soul abilities and aligns with higher dimensional constructs and knowing. This dimension has multiple states and levels within its realm of awareness, including lower fourth, mid fourth, higher fourth, and more. A pivotal realm, it can feel like walking between two worlds until fourth-dimensional energies are anchored and embodied cellularly.

Fifth Dimension (Christ, Light Body): This holds the blueprint and template of wholeness and expression of "perfection." No-thing consciousness: no story, no fear, no-thing to block light energy. There are multiple dimensions beyond this one and all are supporting this movement into the next phase of conscious evolution of humankind. Holding this consciousness does not mean you will not have a body.

Third-Dimensional Influences and Constructs

*If you always do what you've always done,
you will always get what you've always gotten.*
Unknown

Currently, much of the collective whole of society lives influenced by a third-dimensional view of physical reality. In the third dimension, energy is dense and heavy. It is often difficult to work with and it takes significant effort to make changes. Yet things are constantly changing. It is a human, survival, ego-oriented dimension, steeped in a linear and Newtonian-oriented awareness. It is a dimension where many walk around unconscious and unaware of the glory and mystery that lives within them.

People enmeshed in third-dimensional thinking choose to believe that what is happening is *real* and, thus, judgments are made as to what is right and what is wrong. Great meaning is then given to these judgments. It is a reality where people say, "I can't, you have to do this for me." "I am not responsible for what just happened." Thus, the dynamics of a lack of responsibility and accountability for actions abounds.

Additionally, it is a realm of poor me, me-me-me, what I want, being a victim of life and societal and cultural impacting. Yet the adverse ego/small self wants to be in control and, desperately at times, works to be in control through conscious manipulation of events and people. The ego does this in order to be in control, special, and right. Even if being in control, being special, and being right makes them appear as a wounded victim of circumstance.

Third-dimensional expressions are full of resistance and are, collectively, in the midst a resistance epidemic. The resistance is expressed as being wounded, needing to blame others, wanting to project fault on others, and at times even feeling the right to emotionally vomit on others.

People steeped in third-dimensional awareness predominantly see through a fear-based lens and view things in accordance with the prescribed perceptions they have created. Perceptions and beliefs that hold great meaning—and are held and relived in the mind—become embedded as a structure of emotional knowing in the cellular body system and a habitual neural patterning in mind. All meaning-making is created in accordance with the rules and structures of the collective 3D realm. Additionally, as it holds negative-oriented perceptual energies (stress, anger, upset) within the cellular system of the body, over time they create pain in the body.

Third-dimension reality is where people believe they need to know. Know answers, know they are safe, know they are right, and so on. When you believe that there is something that you need to know, that you have a *right* to know, what happens to your body? Your muscles tighten, your emotional reactions often go off the chart, and you become determined to be in control of a person or a situation. You become self-righteous and self-justified. This need to know creates an emotional vibrational resistance within the body system. At every dimensional level you are given a vibrational frequency choice. *Do I choose to make a decision from my currently level of energy—and remain in the status quo—or do I want to make a choice from a higher level and get different results?* You use that choice often and it is always based on the dominant vibration held within your being at any given moment.

Third-dimensional alignment is steeped in the energies that align with fear, sadness, anger, greed, and jealously. These are not wrong or bad emotions; they are simply energy vibrating at a lower frequency. All emotions were initially designed to be influencers and directors of your experiences for making higher choices, but over time you lost this information and began to give these lower survival emotions great meaning based on your personal judgment of what they mean in the moment. You began to see them as something against me, rather than as something that is actually for me—for good.

The third dimension has embedded structures of knowing and rules as a part of its frequency level. Embedded third-dimensional energetic information is rooted in competition, lack, fear, guilt, blame, defensiveness, me-me-me, resistance, linear time, challenge, limitation, and other fear-based limiting perceptions and structures of knowing. Additionally, these perceptions live not only in you as an individual, but also in the collective consciousness. The third dimension holds programmed patterns of meaning regarding relationships: meet someone, fall in love, believe this is the only one. Then comes the controlling, the cheating, etc., all of which are steeped in a construct of conditioned love. Looking for love in all the wrong the places holds this energy in place.

The third dimension firmly holds the constructs of duality—good/bad, right/wrong, judgment based on past perceptions, etc. Thus, you create a future that is determined by these judgments and perceptions. It is a reality steeped in survival and, over time, it has wired your brain for survival as the primary reaction to the experiences of life. This survival mechanism teaches you to look for threats even when there aren't any. Because of this, reaction and resistance are your primary responses. All of this exists because fear rules as the dominant energy in this dimension. The belief in your capacity for choice and self-responsibility are negligible and often overridden by deeply embedded thoughts of fear.

The third dimension holds the embedded patterns of the adverse ego, a.k.a. your small self, the adversary, even the devil. The adverse ego plays small (or extra-large as a bully or power-monger) for it believes it must in be charge of the world to get what it deserves, or that the world or other people will take advantage of them in some way. Our adverse ego/small self rules according to beliefs and perceptions that have been passed down through generations of both personal family and collective society. These beliefs include ideas regarding culture, country, gender, race, and thought-feelings such as *I am not enough, I am not good enough, I do not count, I will always be poor because my family is poor*, and so forth.

The third dimension supports advocacy for change that is steeped in fear, anger, separation of systems and ideals, and force. This includes the desire to change things from a perspective of force that includes threats, war, forcing change, marching in anger, ugly signs depicting words and graphics meant to hurt a group or person, and so much more.

The perception of third-dimensional reality is impacted by all the aforementioned until you are ready to make a conscious choice toward change. This change occurs when you are ready to shift from a fear-based reality to a joy-oriented, elevated-emotion reality. Elevated emotions hold a fourth-dimensional vibration that is more heart-centered, thus they are more coherent, purer, and unconditioned than the lower third-dimension-oriented survival emotions embedded below the heart center.

Example: Elevated Emotions (4ᵗʰ D.) vs. Lower Emotions (3ʳᵈ D.)

Creative 4ᵗʰ D. & Elevated Emotions

Appreciation, Joy, Peace, Trust,	7
Wholeness, Acceptance, Love,	6
Inspiration, Empowerment,	5
Trust, Gratitude, Knowing	4 Selfless

Worry, Guilt, Fear,	3 Selfish
Anger, Doubt, Anxiety	
Insecurity, Shame, Depression	2
Insecurity, Judgement, Hostility,	1
Competion, Sadness, Lust	

Lower Ego-Survival Emotions

Brain research reveals (refer to work by Mark Waldman or Joe Dispenza) that the brain doesn't know the difference between past reality, current reality, or future reality—it is all experienced as *now*.

If every day you relive yesterday's negative events (or the last decade's), you bring all those emotions into the now. And you will be creating vibrational broadcast signals filled with vibrational data that reinforces old habits and negative emotions you hold around them. Then you wonder why life doesn't change for you. It can't change if you don't change it!

The process for this transformation, includes the following (a very short synopsis). First, you *must* agree to "heal." You must say, YES, to transformation and shift! You heal through heart/brain coherence — so, next you are required to get your spiritual, mental, physical, emotional, and thinking bodies/systems aligned. How? Create intentions, stay conscious, engage a spiritual coach, ask empowering questions, forgive, honest self-observation, surrender, engage in sacred service, prayer, meditation, intentional and conscious practices, acts, and actions(gratitude/appreciation), etc. Then, activation through alignment - a heart/brain coherence - will be initiated.

Fourth-Dimensional Influences and Constructs

*The Invisible Realm is real and tangible
to my mind and feelings, now.*
Charles Fillmore, *The 4th Dimension in Man*

The fourth dimension is the initiation into the realm of metaphysics, the realm beyond the physical; it is the bridge between the third and fifth dimensions. Here, you begin to dance with innovative ideas and ways of being and yet you are still dancing between two worlds.

The fourth dimension holds multiple levels of awareness. There are realms such as the lower fourth, mid fourth, and higher fourth. It is in the fourth dimension that you consciously begin the journey into *Soul Mastery* and that the full collapsing of third-dimensional energies, beliefs, and perceptions starts to happen. However, the initial journey begins in the third as you have an awakening or say-YES experience. Here are three of the most common ways that the collapse of the third-dimensional energies occurs:

1. As the spiritual journey into *Soul Mastery* is initiated, the initial awakening begins to cause things to collapse around you, and it appears as if circumstances are forcing you to make a change or to shift—this occurrence may be a divorce, illness, death of a loved one, loss of job, etc. It is a choice point moment: if you don't shift, the suffering of the third dimension continues.

2. As you grow in consciousness and step into higher third dimension, or step into beginning fourth-dimensional awareness, you understand that you have the power to consciously shift situations and experiences. So you consciously make a choice to do so, or not, while holding the highest and best for all involved. And how much you can affect a situation depends upon the level of fear, negative beliefs, etc. that you still hold in consciousness.

3. As you shift into higher levels of dimensional knowing and understanding, your focus is intentional and holds clarity as to the role of energy, vibration, and frequency in demonstrating and shifting situations in your current reality and, thus, you consciously

participate in alchemical transformation and it is an instantaneous experience.

The fourth dimension is akin to a bridge that you must cross over to enter the fifth dimension. However, you do not just blatantly walk across the bridge. You must engage in conscious spiritual growth and awareness on multiple levels of being in order to initiate a movement into fifth-dimensional awareness. Many enter the fourth but get stuck in the entry-level energetic requirements and this halts their progress (for a time or for a lifetime). At the higher-fourth level, you begin to tap more consistently into fifth-dimensional reality.

The fourth dimension holds lighter energy than the third and it is in the lower fourth-dimensional realms that the initiations of release begin. You will begin the release of the old baggage of negative perception, shadows, lower thoughts and feelings—all of which are energy that will be dissolved to be lifted into higher-level vibration.

The lighter fourth-dimensional energy starts to draw things more easily and effortlessly to you. You will process things faster, too! But do not let that fool you. This realm requires constant vigilance, or you will slip back into third-dimensional thinking and ways of being, and you will wonder what just happened. Often it feels as if you are living or dancing between two worlds. And you are!

The fourth dimension is the realm of paradox, polarity-holding, and seeing things from a variety of different perspectives. As a bridge between two other dimensions, the fourth-dimension bridges two different points of awareness or references and you willingly dance with polarities such as knowing/not knowing, wanting/letting go, dark/light, shadow/light, true/not true, sure/not sure, clear/murky, yes/no, and even outdated ideas regarding what masculine/feminine[3] means. You are now a holder or container for the idea of "both/and." As the idea of being a polarity holder comes alive in you, you will notice that you naturally tend to look for multiple creative solutions for issues and that you have released your attachment to the third-dimensional construct of either/or. You know that you are making progress in crossing the bridge when you

---

[3] *Embracing the Feminine Nature of the Divine.* Toni G. Boehm. Inner Visioning Press. Amazon.com

realize that you do not have to make someone else wrong in order to feel right about things.

The fourth dimension is the realm where you are invited to dance at the edge mystery and discover *what is*. As you are unwrapping the meaning of *what is alive in the moment,* you are also learning to energetically perceive and see what isn't interesting as a choice for your life!

Fourth-dimensional awareness is a place of questions, not answers. It is about remembering! You are reminded that what is energetically present in a space can change in a nanosecond. The fourth dimension invites you into seeing all your experiences without judgment, resistance, or attachment. This is the place of unraveling and disassembling old perceptions, beliefs, and attitudes. This disassembling of the old structures of knowing is an imperative of this dimension and must occur if you want to keep your energy light—so continually make conscious choices to stay in vibrational alignment.

Fourth-dimensional awareness initiates a capacity to see the hidden mysteries contained within various religions and spiritual teachings. You will observe them in a new light and context, regardless of whether they are from Buddha, the Master Teacher Jesus, Christianity, Judaism, New Thought, or other venues. As you discover their hidden meaning, you realize the interconnectedness of all spiritual truth and principles.

Fourth-dimensional energy is lighter because you are letting go of old structures of knowing, which frees up energy for new gifts of grace to arise in you that you can use in other areas of your life. These gifts may include intuition, telepathy, being a master facilitator of energy, reading energy fields, seeing auras, third-eye awakening, seeing with more clarity across the dimensions into the past and future, interaction with interdimensional guides and master teachers, and more. As your gifts become more pronounced, they become a constant in your decision-making process. And although your decision and choices must be carried out in the third dimension, they produce outcomes that are better than expected because they have been made from a higher level of awareness.

Fourth-dimensional energy often feels a little like insanity—and it is—for you are in transition, with one foot still in each world. Your ego is breaking down, you are releasing attachments to many things, you are detoxing on many levels as your light body is being activated, you are consciously engaging in seeking out distortions in your emotional field, taking risks of authenticity, you are letting go of the need to be safe and having others assure you that you are safe, you are rewriting your history and that feels discombobulating, and you want to sleep more as your body aches.

You know that your current physical reality is a response to your past and what you hold in consciousness. You start "challenging" karma, for you know it doesn't always have to this way. Multidimensional talents are awakening. You are honoring yourself as the I AM takes dominion of your awareness. The masculine aspects of being surrender to the more feminine[4,5] qualities of being (will, power, etc. surrender to trust, collaboration, cooperation, etc.). Synchro-divinity and synchro-divine events (third-dimensional synchronicities) come into your awareness and become a constant companion.

You begin to process faster and the law of attraction/manifestation comes faster. Abundance starts to flow, and you realize that you are beginning to understand how to connect with the demonstration of it in mind—even though it may still be an initial stage of awareness. You now have the capacity to hold higher-level awareness and elevated emotions for longer periods of times. You notice that you are holding them until you are clear that your vibration is shifting, a new momentum is gathering, and an expansion of consciousness is occurring. Because of all of this, you are willing to do what it takes to clear and live through the initial expression of what feels like insanity.

The fourth dimension consciously awakens the innate aspects and qualities of being that are often thought of as leaning toward the feminine. Feminine aspects can include generosity of spirit, connectivity, interdependence, compassion, connection with the higher emotional intelligence of heart wisdom, the capacity to be conscious of when you are unconscious, the capacity to dance at the

---

[4] *Embracing the Feminine Nature of the Divine.* Toni G. Boehm. Inner Visioning Press. Amazon.com

edge of mystery, to sit in the space of the unknown, and to be comfortable sitting with questions and to not need answers for now, for you are allowing answers to arise from the collective wisdom at hand. You are discovering the capacity to be *Conscious Neutrality* in action, which holds the capacity to neutralize negative energies in your presence—both your own and others. In this neutral and neutralizing consciousness, your need for advocacy shifts from radical anger and force for change to an understanding of the adage: *You cannot solve a problem with the same level of consciousness that created it!* Thus, you BE more creative and peace-oriented in your solution development.

    The fourth dimension is a realm of conscious (and unconscious) clearing and cleansing as you let go of resistance, fight, fear, and more. It is an activation reality, as the first movement into this realm of awareness activates the initial entry of "light energy" into the cellular structures of the body: energy that has been held at bay or hostage, by our fear-based perceptions. As it gathers momentum, this movement of light energy ultimately initiates a massive cellular shift and internal transformation within your being.

    The fourth-dimensional realm is home to the entrance into the unknown and it is where you will begin to feel comfortable with that journey. As you dance at the edge of mystery and dive deep into the interiors of being, dark nights of the ego, dark nights of the soul, shadow exploration, and other opportunities for clearing will occur. (Please note that the word *shadow* is more aligned as a third-dimensional term, for it has much baggage of interpretation associated with it.) These will occur in some form as you are working to activate and integrate the light energy of higher dimensional awareness into the cellular structures and memories of your being. During this phase, it is important to be aware that the process is only as difficult and uncomfortable as you make it through resistance.

    The fourth dimension is a new level of feeling reality. It is not like the third-dimensional projection or owning feelings of anger, jealousy, safety, and so on. In the fourth dimension, it is a feeling of reality where you understand the imperative role that energy, vibration, and frequency (and thought/feeling energy as broadcast signals) have in attracting higher possibility and soul evolution.

The fourth dimension initiates a shift in consciousness that will ultimately move you from awakening to alignment to ascension, and as your understanding of reality shifts at each new level of awareness, you change! Know that this understanding of the movement between dimensions and levels is not a third-dimensional construct of comparison, of comparing how you rank against others; it is a descriptor and a tool for you to utilize in consciously assessing where you stand in each moment.

The fourth dimension initiates a new level of heart opening and feeling/emotional expansion. As your heart wisdom expands, you begin to emit a new vibrational signal, an electromagnetic field that supports alchemical transformation and higher vibrational matching of possibility in the unified field of consciousness. An open, expanded heart also holds elevated emotions, such as appreciation for all experiences, a trust that all is well, that life is just as it should be for the lessons you require, a joy for life, and more. These elevated emotions, each time they arise, release over 1,200 neuro-chemicals in your body, which support you in sustaining a higher field of awareness. And lastly, an open heart and elevated emotions initiate and support the unification process—the unification of various aspects of being (physical, mental, emotional, spiritual)—and as this occurs you collapse old energies and karmic timelines.

Fifth-Dimensional Influences and Constructs

> *My mind is luminous, and I perceive*
> *the luminosity of Spirit everywhere.*
> Charles Fillmore, *The 4th Dimension in Man*

The fifth dimension holds exquisitely pure light energy and vibration. Your emotional and mental bodies are clear, as old beliefs have been released and replaced with this pure, higher, lighter energy—an energy that has established new ways of being and living. Cellular changes are commonplace, as are DNA shifts. It is like the rheostat on your genes has been turned up! Innate capacities that were once hidden are now alive. Instantaneous healing is the norm. This is a very light vibrational state. Being in visible or invisible form is your choice, for here you know life is eternal. In this realm, you consciously connect with all dimensions of the universal and cosmic realms. This is the "New Earth" of *Revelation*.

The fifth dimension is a light-filled, dynamic, vibrant state of aliveness and well-being. It is a realm where you know that no one and nothing is against you or can ever be against you. How could they be? For in this dimension, there is no Velcro of receptivity for resistance. Only ease and grace are alive here. There is nothing to fear, for what can harm you? There is no death! There is only a translation of energy from one dimension to another, and you are connected to all dimensions.

The fifth-dimensional consciousness knows that abundance is the natural state of the universe and is therefore not an issue. How could it be? You have the power of instant manifestation. Every cooperative component you require to manifest all possibility is available to you instantaneously. Energy is malleable and plastic. You know how to work with it in integrity for the highest good of all involved.

The fifth-dimension energy sees easily through all levels of dimensions, for the third eye is clear and fully open. With ease, you read the energy of a room, group, or person when tuned into them. Thus, you read the energetic records of the heart and mind through a highly tuned sense of intuition. This open intuitive facility has the capacity to see/sense what is coming next.

The fifth-dimension energy holds interconnection, interdependence, and cooperation as key elements, and the highest good of all is paramount and understood in a new way. This fifth-dimensional awareness recognizes resistance and resistant energy immediately but does not engage with it. By being in a state of awareness of *Conscious Neutrality*, you have the capacity to consciously neutralize the resistant energy and the energy shifts by simply being in your presence. All things not created from an awareness and choice of truth (things such as manipulation, lies, guilting, control, etc.) are immediately recognized and, not being in alignment with the presence of fifth-dimension energy, are energetically reformed or removed.

In fifth-dimension awareness, all bodies—spiritual, emotional, physical, and—are integrated and functioning as one through clarity of thought and feeling. New values come alive, such as generosity, generosity of spirit, compassion, caring, kindness, integrity, clarity, transparency, authenticity, respect, honor, and inner harmony and resonance. All of which is transmitted through an open heart—some call it love; in higher dimensions, it is known as BE-ing in harmonic resonance with the Universal Impulse.

In fifth-dimensional fields of energy, the following are commonplace: your commitment is to be in service to humanity and, thus, your work is service; being in service to your higher purpose fulfills all your requirements and needs; your soul qualities and talents are active and in service to a greater good; instant manifestation of desires abounds; conscious partnering occurs, both on the inner and outer planes (the inner occurs as divine union and the outer occurs as the capacity to consciously partner with others to co-create higher possibilities for the good of all); an awareness that sees only wholeness and not a need for healing; and an awareness that knows the difference between breaking down and being broken.

In the fifth dimension, growth often emerges through dream states. You start to see inter-dimensionally. You are energetically activated and your words hold the capacity for activation of others through their sound and tones. You know that you cannot act as savior for anyone and you are not here to save another. You understand that the desire to save another is an ego-oriented impulse that believes it knows best and that trying to save someone is trying to save them from their soul work. Your true work is to support others without judgement and the need to save them or spare them.

In fifth-dimensional awareness, you know that you are a soul walking in a body, not a body with a soul. Thus, you see the purpose in all things and make choices moment to moment to observe and refocus on fifth-dimension thoughts and ideals—for you know that you cannot take third-dimensional programmed relationships or ideas into this dimension.

In the fifth dimension, your energy has the capacity to neutralize negativity and for it to happen instantly. You BE *Conscious Neutrality* in action!

Foundational Constructs of Third, Fourth, & Fifth:

Example B is a mini overview of what third-, fourth-, and fifth-dimensional paradigms (patterns or models) and their constructs (ideas, beliefs, perceptions, or theories held within the paradigm) mean in relationship to consciousness and life in general as your energy progresses through the dimensions. This chart will support you in viewing your life from a different perspective.

Review each column, starting with the third dimension. Look for the energetic differences in each dimensional paradigm as it expresses itself in the world and in your life. Ask your inner guide to support you in seeing those areas that are your next steps of soul growth. Take notes on your discoveries.

Example B: Foundational Influences, Behaviors, Actions, & Constructs of Third-, Fourth-, Fifth- Dimensional Realities

Note: a construct is any idea or theory held within a dimension.

Third-Dimensional Constructs	Fourth-Dimensional Constructs	Fifth-Dimensional Constructs
• The construct of 3rd D. reality is fear-based, success-seeking, "me," more, often unaware, unaware of role of TRUE SELF - I AM • Old Earth energy that was prophesied to pass away	• The construct of 4th D. reality moves from seeking to conscious living. • Aware → awakening → awake → alive • 4th D. is bridge between 3rd & 5th D., thus is pivotal and not necessarily stable • 4th D. is path to 5th D. • You cannot do a spiritual bypass on any of the work required	• The construct of 5th D. reality is I AM ONE with living New Earth energy • BE! • Alive → ablaze with luminous energy • Master of energy • Mystery • Unknown/all known • Full surrender to Universal Impulse, the impulse of the ab-SOUL-ute
3rd D. Constructs…	4th D. Constructs…	5th D. Constructs…
• Manifestation is slow, takes time, energy sluggish, dense, is always changing. 3rd D. is impermanent, even though people	• Think and many things appear shortly • Testing consistent giving and tithings to see what happens; still often to receive	• Instant manifestation • Alchemical transformation occurs in their presence • All needs are provided for without worry

believe it is permanent; thus they fear and resist change. • What can I get for what I do, often "gimme!" • Seeks outside of self for kindness, compassion, love, worth, success • Dependent on others for good, love, recognition, status, money • Often lives from lack consciousness, even if they have money and possessions. • Low tolerance for other views, mistakes, etc. • Engages in power struggles • Believes world is against them • Spiritual journey and what is to be met not understood • Judges by appearances and denies their part in creating relationships • Out to get, not necessarily to give • Multidimensionality not believed, ego control imperative • Suppresses feelings • Ego anchored in me • Do it for me, I can't • Must work for money	• Seeking relationship within • Tolerance growing for other views and mistakes • Expressing love, compassion, kindness • Open, yet lives with power struggles • Decreasing need for drama/pain body to be engaged • Conflict management desired and worked at, looks for peace • Basic understanding of spiritual journey and what is to be met • Desires to live from "what IS, IS!" • Invites sacred service and greater giving as a constant into awareness • Spiritually and emotionally evolving • Engages daily spiritual practices • Working "stuff," not through it yet • Optimistic, positive, working to see from 4th D. metaphysical perspective not 3rd D. perception • Works to make conscious choices and take conscious actions • Authentic communication becoming important but still often steeped in my need, my wants	• Knows mystery of Universal Impulse, energy, vibration and frequency, resonant fields, body as field of energy, and their relationship to NOW moment • Knows how to fully work/shift energies • Knows energy of ARC of expression in giving; can't out-give Source • Knows the interconnectedness of all life • Lives consciously and connected to the energy of the unified field of consciousness (UFC) • Knows that in higher awareness, Christ consciousness, there is no fear, no history, no story • Sees only one presence, abundance, and wholeness • Capacity to shift DNA and recognizes when light is luminous or dimming • Understands 5th D. imperatives, infinite possibilities, dimensions, parallel realities, multidimensional aspects • One with UFC, tunes in inter-dimensionally • Works with spiritual masters and guides

• Blame, shame, I need to know why? • I must feel safe • Newtonian cause/effect predicts and controls; linear • Developing or no spiritual practices • Attached to my way, outcomes as they want them; "my will be done" • Fearful of anything unknown • Fear of death • Fear not recognized as leading life and thus, not worked on • Optimistic, pessimistic, drama, my way, my will • Pain body engaged and lived from • Perceptions rule, sees from 3D. perceptions • Makes unconscious choices and takes action from there • Nonauthentic communication; has a need to be right and be sure they are seen as right; thus, conversations often turn negative • Adverse ego is well established • Often fearful of stillness/silence • Often lacks clarity and intentionality	• Engaging eternal life concept but still often a fear of death • Adverse ego hold is shifting • Engaging meditation, stillness, silence • Focus, open, intentional, accountable • Exploring, will take risk • Becoming more comfortable not knowing • Defining self by spiritual parameters • May experience health issues • Duality-One • Knowing one presence, one power (1P-1P) is all there is • Actions motivated by something greater, often not necessarily only for personal gain • Understands intellectually, but knowing not yet grounded • Conveying a level of spiritual wisdom, intuitive insight, etc. that begins cutting through stuck and shadow energy • Experiences moments of divine interludes • Works forgiveness on multiple levels • Desires to live in nonattachment, nonjudgment	• Sees auric fields of color • Matured spiritual ego, I AM, adverse ego overcome • Cooperative components and power required from the UFC are instantaneously available • Energy shifting ability • Can often do the impossible, no fear of anything • Reads energy in space and can shift the energy • Instantaneous results occur along with suspension of time • Clarity regarding abundance; all needs provided without taking thought • Clarity, intentionality, accountability, I AM; integrity of words, actions • Knows "I AM holy" as is "All IS holy!" (Titahquah) • No shadow; knows shadow is illusion and is here to teach who we are and who we are not • Has made peace with "Jesus" and all past religious influences • Understands the hidden blueprint in scriptures as a guide for soul evolution

• Does not want to be held accountable for anything
• Not knowing is very uncomfortable
• Fulfilled/defined by world view
• Actions motivated by hidden motives
• Stuck energy fields
• May experience a divine interlude but often ignores or runs from it
• If a past life bleed-through occurs, not understood, feared
• Controls and constructs of mind firmly in place, as are perceptions
• Drama feeds pain body, which is alive and in place
• Duality-oriented
• Shadow not understood and feared; not looked at; it's always someone else's fault
• Metaphysics feared or toyed with, not engaged in a way that would change the landscape of literal reality
• The calculating self firmly in place
• Not open to feedback and gets upset when feedback given
• Plays games to win	• Realizing everything is impermanent
• Need for control and manipulation decreasing
• Joy in discovering there is nothing to overcome, just opportunities to grow
• Clarity, integrity, and accountability of words and actions are invited into play (and still feared)
• Willingly participating in shadow processes; shadow aspects arise, are reviewed and questioned
• Words and actions beginning to be coherent match, but words often still ring hollow when spoken
• Often engages in metaphysical malpractice and meta-fizzling; i.e. speaks words that are not yet embodied as a living knowing
• Landscape of current reality shifting; often is willing to look, see, tell the truth and shift to something more interesting
• Experiencing déjà vu, past lives, dream-scaping
• Shedding old habits as new values arise
• Understands roles of archetypes/polarity	• Understands Book of Life and accesses it
• Universal law of dominion lived with I AM as fully as dominant vibration of being
• Dances at the edge of mystery, unknown, not knowing; unlearning invited and lived into
• Comfortable in midst of discomfort
• Immortality known, no fear of death
• Activations and initiations are spontaneous
• Understands universe is constantly speaking through synchro-divinity and synchro-divine events to create "success" on our spiritual journey and that S.D. is a sign of resonance with UFC
• Recognizes and bypasses "controls" of mind
• Higher good of all is paramount
• Expresses from transparency and authenticity, invoking law of dominion
• Knows everything is impermanent
• BE and lives Conscious Neutrality with little or no reaction

- Not willing to unlearn, etc. - Unproductive habits not recognized - Shadow aspects intact - Distortion and separation play out in physical body as disease, addiction, me-orientation, etc. - NOTE: We are vibrational beings inviting remembrance to remember why we are here and what we are to do!	- Beginning to understand spiritual journey and obstacles - Symbols, signs, etc., are more important - Dances between dimensions; energy not yet stabilized - Divine masculine (light, knowledge) activates divine feminine (the purifier) to break down old beliefs and structures - Conscious desire and working to cleanse the past - New sensitivity to energy; new skill sets, gifts, and values emerge for use with new life purposes - Distortions of reality being seen; rewiring - Let go need to know - Non-linear - Deep soul work being done, diving deep to expand consciousness - Trusting, honoring self - Ego breaking down - Detoxing of cells - Light body being activated, DNA being restructured - Unconscious programming is decreasing rapidly - Fear is a sign to look, not run; karma collapsing	- Claims, holds, and vibrates in resonance with claim - Knows Kingdom of Heaven is at hand - Holds laser-like intentionality - Experiences interconnectedness and isolation - Soul walking a body - About sacred service, not money or fame; spiritual ego alive - Silence imperative for restoration - Not all bliss; understands this and has no attachment to anything showing up any certain way - Lives nonjudgment, nonattachment, nonresistance - No judgment, therefore, no forgiveness of anyone required - Clarity of multidimensional and interdimensional seeing provides clear energy for viewing life: past, present, future - New Earth realities - In service to humanity - Time ceases - Cellular body clear - New values in place - Secure in self - Unity consciousness is integrated - Whole not healing

	• Metaphysical divine masculine/feminine aspects understood • Heart open to higher levels of awareness • Sexual energy begins to move from lust and need to a desire for a "need to seed" new realities through your creation energy • BE, as a state of awareness, starts to BE initiated in higher 4th D. awareness.	• Creation energy impregnating body with new realities • Intuitive messaging is the norm • Alchemical transformation of energy occurs in your presence • No fear or lack can be sustained in this dimensional awareness • Live in sacred union, unity consciousness

~5~

Mysticism on the Mount & Conscious Neutrality

*Quantum leaps...are evolutionary drivers...
they are vital stimulants which trigger
astounding design innovation.*
Barbara Marx Hubbard (paraphrase)

Instructions from a Master Teacher on How-to BE the Presence of All Is Well and a Master Facilitator of Energy

What is it about the Universal Impulse, Source Energy, God, Spirit, or Universal Intelligence, that when It wants you to do something (and you are aligned with and receptive to Its guidance), It is often relentless in Its energetic nudging? And frequently keeps turning up the energetic heat until you take an action!

It was early spring when I received the first energetic nudge regarding the *Sermon on the Mount*. It wasn't a particularly dramatic or exciting prod. It was just an energetic push, a knowing, that I was to reread the *Sermon on the Mount*. Not being particularly excited about the prospect, my thought was that I would do it in a few days, as I was reading something more interesting at the time.

But after several minutes of relentless pursuit by Spirit, I knew that I had to do it. In fact, within that short span of time, it became an imperative. Spirit is strange like that, at least in Its dealings with me.

What happened when I picked up the Bible and turned to Matthew was unnerving. It was a moment of expansive consciousness and in the midst of it, I began to see energy moving under the words. As the energy moved and swirled, it began to download or imprint new information and data.

It was an invisible vibrational imprint or codex of data that held higher dimensional wisdom, knowledge, and meaning. My work was to recognize its presence and then allow Spirit to unpack its meaning through me.

As I unpacked the data, I began to see that this ancient teaching of the *Sermon on the Mount* was a mystical treatise, a hidden, encoded, mystical teaching on how to BE *Conscious Neutrality* in action, a master facilitator of energy, and a master facilitator of spiritual principle through learning how to work with energy, vibration, and frequency.

Later, I realized that through consistent and continual conscious engagement with the *Sermon's* mystical message that the message was rewiring, redesigning, repatterning, and reforming the neural pathways of my brain. This repatterning resulted in a new state of harmonic resonance and balance—*Conscious Neutrality*—and of BE-ing a vibrational signal of the presence of "all is well."

Over time, I began to realize that this state of BE-ing, once established and demonstrated in consciousness, energetically permeates all actions, words, and thoughts and becomes an energetic force for good.

I now realize that the ultimate culmination of the teaching and subsequent work of the *Sermon on the Mount* is to BE the demonstration of *Conscious Neutrality,* a higher dimensional awareness of spiritual principle in action. *Conscious Neutrality* is the capacity to energetically have command over your emotions; to hold a state of awareness that is in harmonic resonance and balance; and to BE this state of awareness in the midst of all actions you take, regardless of what is going on around you.

In the quadrilogy of the teachings of *Soul Mastery*, attaining the stage of *Conscious Neutrality* also holds the capacity to demonstrate the alchemical transformation of energy—the conscious ability to transform the energy in a space, in a group, or in another person into a higher level of vibration. In *Conscious Neutrality* awareness, you awaken and hone the qualities and elements required for being a master facilitator of energy. And the *Sermon* reveals how to do this!

A Blueprint on How to Expand Consciousness

Two thousand years ago, a man named Jesus came to earth to evolve in consciousness, just like you are doing. Through the events and experiences of his life, he left a blueprint or template for that evolutionary process.

A process that, when understood and seen with *eyes that see*, results in an expansion and ascension in consciousness from a third-dimensional reality expression of consciousness to an expansive connection with multi-dimensions of frequency, knowledge, light, and awareness of fifth-dimensional energies and higher.

Through his evolution, as shared in the Gospels, Jesus embedded in the collective consciousness a template for how to demonstrate the expansion of consciousness; the *Sermon on the Mount* holds an important piece of that template. It is known that the master teacher Jesus, shared over and over, mystical wisdoms and teachings through parable, mystery, and story, and that he left those hidden, mystery teachings for those who were willing to discover how to unlock their hidden messages, mystery, and embedded codes. For many centuries master teachers and students of theology, mysticism, and metaphysics have been working to unravel these codes and mysteries.

In my own research on the *Sermon on the Mount*, the *Sermon* revealed to me a hidden, mystical teaching. It unveiled a portion of the blueprint for the expansion of consciousness into higher levels or dimensions of awareness; along with a step-by-step how-to-instructional curriculum on how to BE a master facilitator of energy, vibration, and frequency. As I see it now, the *Sermon on the Mount*, is a two-part teaching.

Part 1, MT. 1: 1 -17.

Part 1 presents the *end result* of who you will BE energetically and vibrationally, as a new state of conscious awareness (*Conscious Neutrality*) and master facilitator of energy, *after* you do the spiritual and emotional maturing work as outlined in Part 2.

Part 2, MT. 5: 18 - MT. 7: 19.

Part 2 shares a step-by-step, how-to plan on how to release the energetic density and residue of third-dimensional, fear-oriented beliefs and perceptions, held by the adverse ego. It invites, as a teaching, prescribed ways to spiritually and emotionally maturity in order to transform consciousness and BE a master facilitator of energy. Albeit, you must have "eyes to see" the teaching.

Alchemical Transformation and the Sermon

The *Sermon on the Mount*, when seen with *eyes that see*—through the lens of higher dimensional frequencies and awareness—reveals teachings that support you in your personal energetic alchemical transformation. Remember as was stated previously, alchemical transformation is the changing of substance from one form to another while the original substance never changes.

The patterns of form shift (moisture → water → ice) and the substance appears different or changed, but the underlying substance is the same. Thus, an alchemical transformation in consciousness is a movement of energy that creates a vibrational shift into a different level of awareness. That shift in consciousness is out of third-dimensional limitation anchored by the adverse, survival-oriented ego into a greater knowing and realization of who you BE as Christ or illumined-enlightened consciousness.

The information presented here is an attempt to share the results of the alchemical transformation that took place in me as I unwound and unraveled the mystery, wisdom, and instruction of the *Sermon on the Mount*. Thus, the intention of the *Sermon* is to initiate a focused, conscious, orderly, systematic, intentional, progressive, and evolving movement of new ideas and levels of awareness in the mind regarding *Soul Mastery*.

By saying YES to engaging with the energy imbued in the *Sermon*, you are embarking upon a journey, a journey of shift and change. A change in mind, body, DNA, consciousness, experiences, thinking, feeling, and more. Your willingness to participate fully and resolutely has the capacity to alter your life, both internally and externally. The concepts in the *Sermon* clearly reveal how all ideas, life, love, wisdom, peace, abundance, and relationships can be energetically mastered, demonstrated, and manifested in all areas of your life. However, for this to occur, the ideas and principles require engagement in a conscious and orderly way.

The engaging, attuning, and aligning with the key elements, spiritual principles, tenets, ideas, and concepts contained within the

Sermon have the capacity to create a dynamic synergy of transformative energy that supports an expansion of conscious awareness, and alchemically transforms the energy of who you BE.

The Key Elements of the Sermon on the Mount

The tools and practical application ideas found in the *Sermon* are underpinned by four key elements that are a template for developing and demonstrating a higher level of dimensional awareness of spiritual principle. Those key elements are: *BE = Align + Allow + Attract*.

These elements, when rightly understood, are designed to support you in the development of a master consciousness regarding the facilitation of energy in all areas of your life.

The key elements, when used consistently, intentionally, and precisely, result in a repatterning of the neural pathways in the brain. This rewiring supports a sustainable and repeatable demonstration of the spiritual principle or higher awareness that you have established in consciousness, and work regardless of what is appearing in your life.

The key elements *BE = Align + Allow + Attract*, when unraveled through metaphysical interpretation, reveal a how-to template that outlines the shifts in consciousness required to consciously evolve into new dimensions of awareness and, ultimately, mastery of spiritual principle and energy. What might be some the personal changes that will take place in your consciousness as you consciously engage in the work? There will be an alignment to higher dimensional vibrations and frequencies within your entire body cellular system, and this alignment will shake and shift the core of your foundation. There will be shifts in your attitudes, values, levels of expression in relation to spiritual and emotional maturity, ways of BE-ing, and more.

There is no spiritual bypassing! You must do the work! It is the dominant vibration of your BE-ing that determines the level of frequency to which you align. And the template for how to achieve a higher level of alignment is contained in the teachings of the *Sermon on the Mount*. Here is a shorthand version of the *Sermon's* hidden mystical message on how-to to **BE** *Conscious Neutrality* in action:

BE: MT. 5: 1-20.

BE is also referred to as *Conscious Neutrality*.

> **BE** is a state of awareness, a state of consciousness, which is the *end result* of what occurs interiorly as you successfully practically apply and align, sustain ,and maintain in consciousness the teachings found in the key elements of **Align, Allow, & Attract.**

ALIGN, ALLOW, ATTRACT: MT. 5: 21 —> MT. 7: 29

> This segment reveals the how-to teachings which support the development of spiritual and emotional maturity, and the state of BE-ing, *Conscious Neutrality (*and *Mastering Abundance).*

ALIGN:

This element reveals how to **align** consciousness with higher frequencies and dimensions of awareness.

> You do this initially through prayer, meditation, self-observation, forgiveness, letting go, surrender, acceptance of what is, and other conscious practices. Once **align**ed with these higher frequencies, you must then learn how to **allow** them to do their work in and through your energy field.

ALLOW:

You **allow** by being a field of nonresistance (energy).

> By being willing to unlearn everything you thought you knew, being open to doing the deeper inner clearing work presented to you to do and being in conscious surrender to Source Energy. Doing this initiates a deep spiritual and emotional maturing process.

ATTRACT:

Through engaging fully with the energy and dynamics of **align**ing and **allow**ing, you create new fields of vibrational momentum.

> This new vibrational signal and its momentum will begin to **attract** the higher vibrational possibility from the unified field of consciousness.
>
> However, **attract**ion is not enough: you must be willing to take the inspired action, that is rendered through Spirit, in order to bring these possibilities to life. Remember, Universal

Source Energy is an ever-expanding YES vibration and, as such, Source/Spirit doesn't work in terms of big or little ideas. It works vibrationally in terms of how much resistance or nonresistance is present in the field in which It is working.

If you study the metaphysical and mystical key elements, tenets, and principles underlying the *Sermon* and delve deeply into their energetic meaning while practically applying them in your life, your life will change dramatically, you will alchemically transformed. That is a guarantee!

Additionally, the key elements not only hold the key to creating a consciousness of *Conscious Neutrality*, they also hold a foundational understanding of how to master abundance (*Mastering Abundance*).

The mysticism shared in the *Sermon* is a vibrational transmission and a mystical treatise on how to spiritually and mature, in order to BE a master of energy facilitation! Read through these next few pages several times. Absorb the energy and meaning. Don't rush this!

BE = ALIGN + ALLOW + ATTRACT
*Attraction supports action that is in
vibrational alignment with who you BE!*

KEY ELEMENT BE — Matthew 5: 1 - 17

Sermon Introduction and BE-Attitudes

Introduction: Matthew 1: 1-2

1 Now when Jesus saw the crowds, he went up on a mountainside and sat down. His disciples came to him 2 and he began to teach them.

1 Now when Jesus

Jesus, a man, a person just like you and me, a master facilitator of energy, and teacher who innately understood the mystery of and demonstrated the mastery of how to consciously engage the higher dimensional aspects of energy, vibration, and frequency.

saw the crowds

A gathering of negative and lower energetic thoughts and feelings within his being, desiring to arise. Those thoughts that would say – who are you to do this?

he went up on a mountainside

He consciously made a choice to lift and shift his thoughts into alignment with a higher state of energy, vibration, and frequency. Into fifth dimension and multidimensional awareness, where the energy and constructs of "One Presence and One Power" reside.

and sat down.

He surrendered his small-self thoughts, his adverse ego, and allowed an alignment with higher energy and frequencies to shift his thoughts.

His disciples

Energetic fields of thought/feeling within his cellular structure, that have already been prepared and raised into new levels of awareness.

came to him

These prepared centers of consciousness within that are already in alignment with higher awareness and frequencies, support an alchemical transformation of lower energies and a movement into alignment, attunement, and harmonic resonance with the "Christ" vibration. A vibration that is always present in your field of awareness.

2 and he began to teach them...

BE-ing in a state of alignment, Jesus was receptive and began to receive new downloads of light/information, which his centers of energy/consciousness/awareness were receptive to receive. Aligned to higher vibrations and frequency, the Universal Impulse moved through him and created an expansion of consciousness within the entirety of his BE-ing.

Beatitudes – BE-Attitudes Matthew 1: 2-17
BE!

The *Sermon* is a mystical teaching that holds a timeless blueprint for instructions on how to BE a master facilitator of energy through the development of; spiritual and emotional maturity, spiritual mind discipline, vibrational alignment, non-resistance, demonstration of spiritual principle in consciousness, and the state of awareness referred to as, *Conscious Neutrality*.

BE!

BE in alignment and harmonic resonance, in both consciousness and the cellular structure of the body, with higher and multidimensional levels of energy, vibration, and frequency.

BE a walking field of higher energy that is both felt, observed, and perceived by others that encounter your field.

BE in alignment and coherence with elevated thoughts and elevated emotions/feelings that create a dominant field of energy, known as a vibrational resonance or broadcast signal (VBS), that attracts the highest possibility in the unified field of potential available.

Attitudes

Energetically speaking, **Attitudes** refer to a demonstration in consciousness of fourth- and fifth-dimensional principles and information, which leads to new awareness's and a transformation of BE-ing. A transformation that leads to a state of BE-ing called, *Conscious Neutrality*. In the presence of this field of higher vibrational awareness, an energetic influence takes place, alchemical transformation occurs, and human dynamics shift.

2 He said: Blessed are...

Bless, metaphysically means to confer energy as the activity and action of God/Spirit in motion and to consciously increase and multiply its capacity for working for the higher good for all.

Bless, if "bless" means to confer energy upon, consider what type of energy you might be blessing your life with. Is it a blessing of conferring the energy of resistance, or higher dimensional activation? The law works: right use or reverse use, the law works!

Are, a statement of completion, already done, established, AS one in this state of awareness.

NOW, vibrationally, AS you are this walking, talking energetic state of Blessing, you are consciously conferring the energy of God activity in action toward increase and multiplication, in every interaction you engage in.

Blessed are, those who BE in an increased state of higher dimensional awareness and who hold the energy and luminosity of truth in their vibration field – as in this state of BE-ing, wherever they go, that higher vibration confers Its energy to others of like resonance and/or who are receptive to It.

Blessed are those who BE an increased speed of vibration, as they NOW carry (are cellularly immersed in) an energetic vibrational field of higher truth, luminosity, and light and they confer that energy upon all they come into contact with,

Blessed are those who BE a master of energy for they have the spiritual principles required to perform energy work at higher levels and dimensions of awareness. In this state of *Soul Mastery*, there is now a demonstrable, ever-present, repeatable, and sustainable energy available. And it is instantaneous when called upon in the moment. Once the establishment of the demonstration of a spiritual principle (e.g., abundance) in consciousness is established, it is sustained because new neural patterns have been rewired into the brain's neural pathways and they now serve as the brain's default mechanism.

3 Blessed are the poor in spirit, for theirs is the kingdom of heaven.
>**Blessed are**
>
>NOW, vibrationally you BE the energy of God activity in action moving all things toward increase and multiplication.
>
>**the poor in spirit**
>
>Those who are surrendered, who are willing to seek and do the will of Universal Presence/Spirit/Source/ Energy/ Invisible Intelligence.
>
>**For theirs is**
>
>Theirs IS NOW and they are NOW aligned with.
>
>**The kingdom of heaven**
>
>Heavens, higher dimensional awareness, the unified field of consciousness, container and connector of all potential and possibility worked upon through the activity of law.

4 Blessed are those who mourn, for they will be comforted.
>**Blessed are those who mourn**
>
>To mourn is to desire, long for, and cry out for an expansion of higher dimensional understanding and awareness of who we BE. Those who cry out and long with all their being for an expanded sense of knowing God/Spirit/Universal Presence are compelled by an energy or desire for Universal Awareness. Blessed are those who cry out saying, "I know that I don't know, but Spirit knows."
>
>**for they will be comforted.**
>
>Before you call, I will answer; ask and you will receive the resources required to be comforted. You will be guided to sources and resources in order to be alchemically transformed and to gain higher dimensional awareness, energy, joy, etc. Which is the true treasure.

5 Blessed are the meek, for they will inherit the earth.
>**Blessed are the meek**
>
>The meek, the humbled, those who have energetically discovered and overcome the needs of the adverse or lower ego. The needs that show up as the desire to be first or "me first." Those who understand sacred service as a state of being—sharing their

talents and time—not to be seen or heard but for the glory of food for all.
For they will inherit the earth.
They will embrace a new vibrational level of awareness about who they BE, within their field of energy.

6 Blessed are those who hunger and thirst for righteousness, for they will be filled.
Blessed are
Bless IS one who IS NOW the energetic vibrational field of a higher truth and awareness.
Those who hunger and thirst for righteousness
Hunger and thirst: those who ask, long for, and live from an unquenchable desire for expanded awareness of consciousness.
For they will be filled.
They will BE higher awareness in action, *Conscious Neutrality* in action, and a master facilitator of energy and spiritual principle.

7 Blessed are the merciful, for they will be shown mercy.
Blessed are
One who IS NOW the energetic vibrational field of a higher truth.
The merciful
Those who are willing to forgive, energetically releasing resistance, and a negative force field.
For they will be shown mercy
They will send forth a new vibrational signal into the unified field of consciousness that will return to them greater good.

8 Blessed are the pure in heart, for they will see God.
Blessed are
One who IS NOW the energetic vibrational field of a higher truth.
The pure in heart
Those receptive to purer, clearer, higher vibrations and frequencies. Those who hold pure and intentional energy for highest good of all to be shared and expressed. Those who have

overcome the lower vibrational energy fields anchored in the third dimension: fear, anxiety, me first, playing small, greed, jealousy, insecurity, etc.

For they will see God.
They will be a higher vibrational awareness in action. You are the place where God IS expressed in the world, you are God in expression; those who see you see the energy of God expressing or not!

9 Blessed are the peacemakers, for they will be called children of God.

Blessed are
One who IS NOW the energetic vibrational field of a higher truth.

The Peacemakers
One who has raised consciousness to a state of *Conscious Neutrality* and stands as the presence of "all is well," regardless of what is happening in the space! And as the presence of truth energy – energy shifts and is transformed.

For they will BE called children of God.
They will BE recognized and acknowledged in the higher realms as one in alignment with I AM, the higher awareness of BE-ing, not necessarily in the realm of the third dimension. For in the third dimension, their gifts and talents may be misperceived and not recognized.

10 Blessed are those who are persecuted because of righteousness, for theirs is the kingdom of heaven.

Blessed are
One who IS NOW the energetic vibrational field of a higher truth.

Those who are persecuted because of righteousness
Persecuted, misunderstood energetically, not seen for positive, higher awareness and energy field that they carry; in fact, they are rejected because of it. Righteousness is "right" energy, having aligned with a higher awareness. This may even be revealed an internal struggle with small self – who do you think you are? You are not worthy!

For theirs is
They NOW resonate harmonically with the greatest riches, the gift of higher frequency awareness.
The kingdom of heaven.
Higher dimensional awareness.

11 Blessed are you when people insult you, persecute you, and falsely say all kinds of evil against you because of me.

Blessed are you
One who IS NOW the energetic vibrational field of a higher truth.

When people insult you, persecute you, and falsely say all kinds of evil against you because of me
Often, people – including your own internal critics and "thought people," – do not resonant with the energy field that you now BE. They do not harmonically resonate with the energy, they fear and misunderstand it, are fearful of it and thus, reject it – and you.

12 Rejoice and be glad, because great is your reward in heaven, for in the same way they persecuted the prophets who were before you.

Rejoice and be glad, because great is your reward in heaven
Regardless of appearance, of how people treat you, stay focused and intentional. BE energetically and harmonically in resonance with truth, for that is where true joy and satisfaction reside.
The reward of choosing to stay in the state of *Conscious Neutrality* is an expansion of the vibration and frequency of the consciousness of truth that is anchored and stabilized the more you consciously work with it.

For in the same way they persecuted the prophets who were before you.
Other master facilitators of energy who have come before you have had these experiences and have persevered in the higher realms.

BE Salt and Light
MT. 5: 13-16
13 You are the salt of the earth.
Salt means energy of truth: You are the energy of truth in expression and you must be vigilant to stay in that consciousness, for without truth as the expression in consciousness, nothing you say or do impacts your field or the fields you play in.

14 You are the light of the world.
Light means higher frequency, awareness, holder of information, and energy in motion. When you are aligned in a higher level of light frequency, It cannot be hidden for It is a radiant, luminous energy.

That luminous energy will express Itself in a multitude of ways, such as transforming your current landscape of reality and the energy in every cell of your being as It radiates out through your energy field.

People will sense It: some will be attracted to it and some will reject it out of fear without understanding why they are rejecting It.

BE Higher Righteousness and Fulfillment of the Law
MT. 5: 17
17 I have not come to abolish the Law ... but to fulfill it.
To **fulfill the law** means to raise the level of energy, the field of vibration in which you live, move, and have your being, in order that you may BE a state of awareness that effects change by virtue of your presence. Righteousness means "energy that has been made right, lifted to new states of vibrational awareness." You BE "right energy" when you shift your awareness from third-dimensional constructs to higher levels of awareness. You currently reside in third-dimensional constructs that are steeped in fear, anger, greed, conditioned love, etc., and the work is to raise your vibrations in order that you may BE a vibrational force field of higher dimensional awareness.

The BE-Attitudes are the fulfillment, they reveal the end result of who you will BE once you do the work to release the hold that the third-dimensional adverse-ego, with its false beliefs and perceptions, has on you. The adverse ego, a third-dimensional construct, holds you hostage to its wants, its justifications, its need to be right and to be seen as right, but as you begin to grow into higher dimensions of vibrational awareness, that egoic hold begins to dissolve.

As you ascend in awareness, the veils of egoic illusion dissolve, and who you BE begins to alchemically and energetically transform. You shift energies and vibrationally start to BE the tenets of the Beatitudes. You BE "poor in spirit," "meek," "a peacemaker," and more. You alchemically transform the lower states of limited, adverse-egoic awareness into new dimensions of understanding.

Alchemical transformation is a scientific principle regarding how certain substance change and transform when different frequencies are introduced into them. As the frequency changes, the substance transforms. And so it is with us. As we shift our perceptual energies by raising our vibration and frequency, we begin to alchemically transform interiorly. New dimensions of awareness awaken ideas and perceptions that change who we BE.

In this state, you BE (are now) a receptive energy field of multidimensional awareness, a state of being that higher frequencies move through effortlessly, as long as you remain in alignment. In this higher state of vibrational being and awareness (fourth- and fifth-dimension orientation), you are a blessing. And the energy of truth goes forth, through you, to do its alchemical work of transforming the energy in a space for the highest good of all involved.

In this state of higher energy, you *BE* the presence of truth energy wherever you go. People feel it and that truth energy has the capacity to shift, lift, influence, and transform the energy present in the space. You become an influencer of the energetic field, not just yours but others', through the connections and alignment alive in the unified field of consciousness.

When you BE this energy, you KNOW It works in and through you. You BE a whole new state of awareness that holds the following qualities and values:

> **BE** *a state of awareness that holds higher dimensional energy, vibration, and frequency with ease and grace*
> **BE** *Conscious Neutrality (harmonic resonance) in action*
> **BE** *authentic, BE transparent, BE clarity, BE intentional*

> ***BE*** *focused intention, BE self-observant, BE surrendered*
> ***BE*** *willing, BE humbled, BE receptive, BE integrity*
> ***BE*** *non-resistant, BE non-attachment, BE non-judgment*
> ***BE*** *diverse, BE inclusive, BE appreciation, BE alignment*
> ***BE*** *allowing/receptivity, BE God's will in action*
> ***BE*** *attraction guided by inspired spiritual action*
> **BE** self-observant, *BE appreciation in action*
> **BE** *peacemaker, BE expansive consciousness*
> ***BE*** *. . .* these qualities and values expressing!

In the context of life today, a question facing mystics and those who BE a master of energy facilitation is, "What energies and vibrations are influencing my every thought, and are they serving the highest good for all?"

Remember, the *Sermon* says, "Every penny (thought) will be accounted for!" What energy influences you when it comes to life, political, and/or social justice issues? Third-dimensional mass consciousness, with its fears and protests and judgments? Or the higher-level energies that know that spiritually oriented persons shift energy in different ways?

Third-dimensional mass consciousness tends to stand in protest, in resistance—egoically, righteously, and justifiably fighting for justice and causes—whereas the spiritually oriented critical mass supports spiritually inspired intuitive actions that influence alchemical transformation, a transformation that arises from being aligned to and in connection with the unified field consciousness at a higher level of dimensional awareness.

Actions from this level often look weak to the uninitiated, for these actions appear to be passive. It is like holding a high watch, organizing like-minded people to sit together in meditation at a precise time and with a single focus. Or writing a letter that clearly states in a state of nonresistance and non-defensiveness what you want to happen, not what you don't want to happen.

These actions may appear to the outside world that you are passively doing nothing, when in fact through alignment (prayer, meditation, self-observation, precise and pristine holding of elevated thoughts and emotions, intentional focus on higher levels of alignment, appreciation of Higher Power, knowing what you don't know, etc.) you are influencing the unified field of consciousness around you.

Remember, the Kingdom of Heavens is entered through the *narrow gate* (ascended vibrational consciousness and awareness), not the gates of the masses (lower vibration). Consider the fall of Communism in the USSR and the downing of Berlin Wall in Germany. The collapse of these entities did not happen through war but through the organizing of a few like-minded people around a concept of a harmonic convergence, a World Day of Peace. Hands Across Peace inspired spiritual critical masses to take action together in an alignment of a single intention and focus for peace.

Thus, ends the BE segment of this dynamic mystical teaching. The ultimate culmination of the work of the *Sermon* is to BE the demonstration of *Conscious Neutrality*. *Conscious Neutrality* is the capacity to hold a state of awareness that is in harmonic resonance and balance—regardless of what is going on around you. To BE *Conscious Neutrality* in all the activities you engage in and in all actions you take.

In the quadrilogy of the teachings of *Soul Mastery*, attaining the stage of *Conscious Neutrality* initiates the building of the capacity to demonstrate the alchemical transformation of energy—the conscious ability to transform energy in a space, in a group, or in a person into a higher level of vibration. In *Conscious Neutrality* awareness, you begin to awaken the qualities and elements required for being a master facilitator of energy and to master abundance.

KEY ELEMENT ALIGN — *Matthew 5: 21- 48, Matthew 6: 14*

The key elements of **Align, Allow, & Attract**, as found in teachings of MT. 5: 21 through MT. 7: 29, are the how-to of the *Sermon*. They are the foundational how-to teachings supporting how-to develop the state of BE-ing, *Conscious Neutrality*.

Align/Alignment
 Alignment – First and foremost, realize that what you choose to focus on—positive thoughts and feelings or negative thoughts and feelings—will determine the rate and level of awareness and frequency you align with.

Alignment to higher levels of vibration and frequency is accomplished through meditation, prayer, exercising spiritual mind discipline over thoughts and emotions, self-observation, creating balance and a harmonic resonance within being, etc. (Refer to *A&A, Soul Mastery Soul-utions*.)

Meditation increases vibration and decreases resistance while releasing the hold of the adverse ego. It also increases your capacity for alchemical transformation and opens you to a higher level of receptivity to new ideas.

Meditation aligns you with higher dimensional values such as transparency, accountability, clarity, cooperation, honest self-observation, connection, willingness, nonattachment, nonresistance, etc. You must BE these qualities and values, for they support the transformation of your shadow and other third-dimensional energetic dynamics.

Anger, Murder, Reconcile Quickly, and Release on the Altar
MT. 5: 21-26

Murder, anger, and contempt are third-dimensional energetic fear-survival oriented constructs that eventually must be transformed into higher levels of awareness. This takes spiritual mind discipline and the capacity to release ego needs to put God first.

To surrender to the highest possibility for the greater good of all, you must nevertheless BE willing even if you don't want to! Reconcile these energies, lift them, transform them. Twice, the master teacher refers to the idea of going into the "secret chamber of the heart" to pray. To pray is to consciously align with the higher energies of Source. And yet before you do this, you need to do the following:

Leave your gifts. Leave your desires and your vibrational requests at the altar and seek first reconciliation of your own negative energies. Before you ask for your good, you need to be in a surrendered place, willing to align to higher energy and to invite a new energy that is focused, intentional, nonresistant, unattached, nonjudgmental.

Forgive. Give for: align with a new harmonic resonance, align with a new energy, and give that energy forth instead in the face of perceived wrongdoing. And you can't do it just a little or just what you want to do. All must be aligned (the last penny given, no shred of energetic animosity toward anyone or anything).

Settle matters quickly. Soften your hard-stand vibrations of anger and upset and do it quickly, for the longer you hold onto the energetic strands of lower vibrational thoughts and feelings, the more potential they have to create habitual ruts in your neural pathways—ruts that become embedded beliefs and perceptions that unconsciously rule your life and hold you hostage.

And there is no stronger prison than your mind when it is stuck in the muck and mire of adverse ego perception, a perception that believes that someone or something is against you!

Freedom starts from within; it does not happen because of conditions occurring in the outer world. Freedom is an inner-world process.

Last penny paid. You cannot energetically pretend to have released the lower vibrational hold of negative thoughts and feelings. You must let go and BE a clean energetic slate.

Have no resistance: BE a place of focused intentionality for the greater and highest good of all, not just self.

Adultery and Right-Eye, Right-Hand Release
MT 5: 27-30

To **commit adultery** energetically means to make a conscious choice in the moment to move away from balance and alignment with Source Energy and awareness to appease ego needs of being right, seen as being right, being first, being angry, not being transparent or authentic, playing small so others feel sorry for you, and so on. It also, metaphysically means, to water down the truth of things, in order to do things "my" way.

There is an energetic subtlety here that is important to mention about adultery. It is a deeper and more subtle idea in regard to the moving away from the alignment and balance with Universal Source Energy.

It is a subtle reference to your interior masculine and feminine energies and a reminder that they must always be in balance (and conscious interplay) with each other. Neither one can be able to dominate, regardless of your gender.

Remember these two things:

First, Jesus was teaching in mystery, only to be understood by those who had *ears to hear, and eyes to see*, those who were in higher dimensional awareness, (not the scribes and Pharisees, who believed they already knew)!

Second, there was neither the language nor the understanding to speak of these things in the same capacity that we have today.

Adultery occurs when the **right eye/right hand** misuses or abuses its birthright of truth (right refers to masculine energies and left refers to feminine energies) or when masculine aspects of being shun or move out of balance with their feminine counterparts and qualities (compassion, integrity, transparency, authenticity, connection, "both/and," etc.).

We speak of *one* or *oneness*, but for sacred union to occur, the masculine and feminine energetic qualities of being must be in harmonic resonance and balance.

Charles Fillmore said in 1916, "Jesus Christ reached the limit of his masculine consciousness. He was the heat of world, the light of the world, but he could not be this heat and light ... he had to take on his Divine Mother consciousness. We have not yet the understanding of this Divine Mother consciousness."

And we too, must take on the divine mother consciousness!

This is an imperative in the evolutionary process and in the cycle of conscious evolution.

Do not dismiss this or spiritually bypass it.

Right eye, **right hand**, and **choose quickly**. As you practice self-observation, you will begin to notice when you are vibrationally out of alignment, when you are not focused on higher awareness. When your thoughts are straying (right eye or right hand), it is imperative for you to observe that you are out alignment and then quickly make a conscious choice to realign. For one thought leads to another and, before long, if you do not take care of negative thinking and feeling quickly, you will be steeped in negative patterning.

Divorce and Marrying a Divorced Woman
MT 5: 31-32

Divorce energetically pertains to the feminine and masculine natures of the divine. Your work as part of the process of evolution is to experience the sacred union of the masculine and feminine aspects of being (refer to the wedding at Cana for more insights on sacred union).

However, at times the feminine energy of compassion, authenticity, and transparency can get in the way of your ego's agenda, so you divorce from it and do what you want. Your feminine energies are scorned and set aside.

The feminine is often referred to in the following manner: *Who needs emotion? They just make you seem weak! Don't cry, it is not seemly.* However, when you are overly sensitive, get hurt easily, go overboard with your sense of compassion, act like you are victim of someone else's projections of thoughts, etc. you have divorced the strength of your feminine nature. The feminine nature is soft, and it is also fierce, when it needs to be. But one must be in balance, in order to know how to effectively wield these energies.

This last part is subtle: **anyone who marries a divorced woman commits adultery**. If you join in union with lower emotions -- lower survival emotions, which represent the unhealed aspects of the feminine nature and also emotion divorced from truth of being – and allow them to run your life, and you consciously do not work with them to try to reconcile or raise them—or you deny your emotions have any place in your work or life—then you are divorcing the feminine. All of which takes you out of balance. Not good: they will become part of your shadow!

These negative, out of balance energies will become embedded in your cellular system and support you in staying in a sense of third-dimensional separation—and **adultery** is separation from Source, being out of alignment with Source Energy, or not in harmonic resonance or balance.

Oaths and Retaliation
MT. 5: 33-37

Oaths. Energy is always shifting and changing, therefore do not say "ever" or "never," for you don't know what will be asked of or required of you. Stay focused and intentional on raising your energy and making choices based on what is making itself known in the moment. Swear to nothing, for you know nothing. Really, you don't. You only have perceptions in the moment and everything changes so quickly, so how can we be sure of anything? Dance at the edge of mystery through knowing, "I know that I know nothing!"

Retaliate. Don't do it. It is a lower dimensional reaction and it always reaps bad karma. One living from the state of awareness of *Conscious Neutrality* knows what this means. Non-retaliation, or non-resistance, as an act of real and true power, can only occur when you have command over your emotions and responses.

Let your yes be yes. Two thousand years later and this is an incredible expression of how to imprint upon the unified field of consciousness and the energetic field of substance. When we imprint upon the field, as we do with clarity and intentionality, we are working with the law to bring forth the highest possibility that we are vibrationally in alignment with.

Eye for Eye, Go the Extra Mile, and Give
MT. 5: 38 - 42

Eye for an Eye. BE nonresistance in action, **give** love for ____, and go the extra mile in times of perceived persecution and peace; no more needs be said.
Check to see if your ego didn't like that.
Did it throw up any resistance such as, *"But what if? You don't understand this situation!"*
There is your clue! Resistance breeds more resistance.
You cannot expect to sow resistance and grow love!

Love for Enemies, Pray for Those Who Persecute You, and BE Perfection in Action
MT. 5: 43 - 48

Love your enemies. Energetically, this means seeing all persons as people who are working to open their hearts to find their soul. They are doing the best they can with the energy level they are currently working from. This doesn't mean you never take action, but be assured that it is inspired action not an action that holds pity, anger, or a need to save them from themselves. They are where they need to be in order to learn what their soul is inviting them into.

Piety and Giving to the Needy, Do All in Secret, Know God Will See and Reward You
MT. 6: 1-4

Do not practice righteousness in front of others. The teacher says this several times in a variety of ways. So take heed of the message. Humility! Practice it, practice it, and practice it some more, until it becomes a natural state of BE-ing.

Give in secret. Do not brag about what you have done or given to so and so. Be benevolent, be giving, be without words.

Wordy prayers mean nothing; the real question is, "Are you aligning with the luminous light, the dynamic energy within?"

Wordy prayers are their own **reward**, and **the reward of secret prayer** is that substance and light sustain it. You need the communion and union with the higher realms of being to tap this light.

Your greatest gifts come from silent sacred service, not from being seen for your service.

For it is not you or I who does the work, but the energy of the Universal Impulse, the Universal Intelligence, or the God moving through you.

When you do your deeper work, establishing a new foundational construct for the ascension of the needy aspects of you, there is no need to shout it from the rooftops.

Just do your **work in secret,** for there will be **your reward** and your reward will be that you will rise in conscious awareness, vibration, and frequency and you will be transformed.

Prayer and Fasting, Go into Your Closet and Pray in Secret, and Father/Source Knows What You Need Before You Ask   MT. 6: 5 - 8

As you go into the **inner room/inner closet** and **close the door**/leave all else behind—meaning as you enter the inner realms or inner dimensions — enter, bringing only the dominant vibration of your spiritual identity/I Am. Leave all other thoughts/feelings/emotions behind.

This key element, **Align**ment, initiates the sacred secret journey to the interior of self – and it is dome through prayer and meditation. Start by going within without any agendas. Leave them all at the door, on the altar. Pray for nothing, no-thing, once you go inside. Issues don't exist in the fifth dimension anyway.

Meditation culminates in touching the stillness, even for just the briefest of moments. It is a dynamic state of mind or consciousness, that appears passive, that supports tuning in and aligning with Source Energy. It is an alignment or focus of intentional energy toward higher dimensional awareness.

Alignment supports you BE-ing in harmonic resonance with the Source of your BE-ing, higher universal energies, which are always available to you. And as you do this, the energies will teach you, more and more, how to BE in every moment.

All methods that bring you into contact with God are appropriate. Pray until you set up UNION with the ONE MIND, at which time the Universal Impulse will course through you and ideas will flow, concepts will be understood, energy fields become like books you can read, synchro-divine events will begin to occur spontaneously, around you, and you will synchronize with the energy of the inner quality of everything.

The Father/Source Energy knows what you need, before you ask, so concentrate on **Align**ment, and the Universal Presence will create synchro-divine events to meet all your needs.

Per Charles Fillmore, as you pray and as you bless, you tap into and touch the inner forces of the natural world, especially the element energies and forces of the inner worlds (and through this, you have the capacity to alchemically transform things). With the loaves and fishes, Jesus tapped into the substance of their inner forces, for the inner forces of the electrons of two fish and five loaves were Spirit.

If you have this understanding of the mind, of the dynamic power blessing and prayer and of the mind to open the atomic structure of everything, you begin to see how Elijah started the never-ending oil supply for the widow. How Jesus took the young boy's fishes and loaves and expanded their substance. And how Jesus was able to rearrange the cellular structure of body and ascend into the heavens. You can do this too, for all these things were done under the law and through the law of blessing. They came through the understanding of the dynamic power of blessing and prayer.

In entering that inner closet, Jesus felt the dynamic power and energy of Spirit—*the action of God, the energy of God moving* — moving in him. He knew the law. *God is Spirit and they that worship him must do so in Spirit and truth.*

What is it that stops you from doing this? It is because of the adversary/the adverse ego/the small self. You have incorporated into your brain and body cells the energy of the adversary, the third-dimensional belief in fear, lack, limitation, not being enough, etc. When you start your journey into *Soul Mastery*, the adversary, those shadow aspects of self, must dissolve in order to ALLOW more Light into the cellular structure. The hell and agony that the third-dimensional shadow, and its perceptual constructs bring, must be left behind, dissolved into the nothingness that they are.

The process is like the chrysalis and the butterfly: To transform, the butterfly must kick and squirm out of the chrysalis and no one else can help. You must understand what is happening and do it yourself. Getting rid of old perceptions and the shadows that they have created is challenging work. It is not just platitudes and wishing it away or faking it until you make it.

Jesus went through a journey of spiritual evolution and of spiritual mind discipline, etc. just as you must do. He preceded you, and all of humankind, in soul evolution, evolving out of the old and into the new being in higher awareness: Christ consciousness.

The greatest factor in *Soul Mastery* is prayer. God is omnipotent, ALL power, but it is you who must release that power through and into your cells and being. Prayer is tapping into a higher principle and power to bring it into expression. In your prayers, in your concentration, in your meditation, silence, and speaking of affirmation, consciously desire to connect to the ONE source of being.

Pray in this Way, The Lord's Prayer
MT. 6: 9-13

Matthew 6:9 initiates the Lord's Prayer, with words similar to this; pray in this way. However, in the original Aramaic, the word underpinning that sentence is Beshemi. According to Aramaic scholar, Neil Douglas Klotz, the root word of Beshemi is Shem. Shem means, light, sound, vibration, or frequency. So, in light of today's Aramaic scholarship and interpretation, that sentence might now read; **BE** in **Align**ment with the Light, and Vibration of the Energy of this prayer.

KEY ELEMENT ALLOW — MT. 6:14 - 7:6

Now that you are energetically **align**ed, the work is to learn how to consciously and continually release resistance and to engage effortlessly and consistently with the higher vibrational energies of who you truly BE. Developing the capacity to **allow** might be the most important instructional demonstration you can learn. Why?

Because you can meditate and align every day, but if you get up and go out into the world and **allow** discordant energy to create negative reaction within you, you have just negated all of the energy work you did in meditation.

When you **allow** Universal Presence/God/Spirit to be the leading vibration in your personal energy field, the law of dominion (dominant vibration)/the law of vibrational attraction then goes forth into the unified field to match with the highest possibility that is in alignment with your dominant vibration. And that possibility is then translated into a tangible manifestation in your life!

BE a harmonic resonant field of pure energy in expression.
BE the space of non-resistance, non-attachment, non-judgement.

There are tools that support the development of the capacity for allowing, and several are shared in this segment of the *Sermon on the Mount.* This whole section is a discourse on being aware of what you **allow** to influence your state of being as a dominant vibration. You were given freewill. It is always your choice as to what you align to and what you allow to impact your life and energy field. Remember, one who lives in a state of *Soul Mastery* is a master facilitator of energy and, thus, stays alert to the energy in a space and consciously makes choices that invite higher-level (not lower-level) vibrations in.

It is said that to be a master of a subject takes 10,000 hours of apprenticeship and discipline development. *Soul Mastery* requires that plus a consistent and conscious realignment of your frequencies repeatedly in each moment. Your words (thoughts and emotions) have power. *Soul Mastery* closes the gap of incoherence when you consider the following:

- Are you focused on what you want or are you focused on what you don't want?
    - Thinking you are focused on what you want BUT speaking about what you don't want? "I am abundant—but no way will it happen!"
    - Resistance stops the flow, remember this!
- Are your words (thoughts-emotions) vibrationally accurate?
- Are they in alignment with what you say you want?
- Split energies—wanting one thing and focusing on and speaking to why you can't have it—create a state of incoherence. Nothing good happens in this state.

<u>Forgive and Fasting</u>
MT. 6: 14 -18

> **Forgiveness** has nothing to do with an outer act. This has to do with a state of inner being. Regardless of what occurs, BE a state of nonresistance, nonattachment, nonjudgment, *Conscious Neutrality*, and that energy will work in accord with the law to support you in all your endeavors. Right use or reverse use, the law works!
>
> This is not talking about abusive situations and enduring physical abuse from another. No, this is about having the inner strength to walk away from the situation without blaming the other person. I am leaving because it is best for

me, not because of another's faults or behaviors. Can you see the subtle difference there?

Fasting when you are engaging in energetic healing practices: don't brag about how good you are or what good fortune you are receiving because you are doing it so right. **Fast**, use little amounts of words. **Allow** your presence to **BE** what is seen. And **BE** present to the energy in the field around you, regardless of what you are doing or whom you are engaging with. If you notice that energy is discordant, you can **in secret**—without a word—begin to consciously shift and alchemically transform the discordant energy by virtue of your presence. This means you do not make a big deal out of your spiritual practices or gifts. Yes, you have them—so use them.

By **fasting** from bragging or engaging in egoic behaviors, you become known by your fruits/good energy, and that is the real **reward**. So you don't have to tell everyone how good you are; higher energy speaks for itself.

Anxiety, Treasures in Heaven, Eye Lamp of Body, and You Cannot Serve Two Masters
MT. 6: 19 - 24

Treasure: Where your thought-feeling energy (**treasure**) is focused (on lower or elevated energies) determines the energy you bring to a space and how you engage with others. For **where your heart** is reveals your state of emotions (survival-egoic or elevated). Energy doesn't lie!

If your energy is not in a higher level of harmonic resonance (**your treasure**), people will hear it in your words, see it in your actions, and they will know that something is not quite right. And if they are sensitive, they will know that incoherent energy is present. Even if you think you are doing a great job of faking it, know you are not!

Eye Single: BE-ing a master of energy facilitation requires that your **eye be single**, that you develop a single-focus consciousness, a laser-like intentionality and generosity. The **eye** is how you see and perceive things in life. Do you see through **dark**, unhealthy (cynical, defensive, etc.) **eyes**?

Or do you see through **healthy eyes** filled with **light**, which see all is for good, regardless of appearance?

You cannot serve two masters. The Universal Impulse/nonphysical, pure positive energy/Christ consciousness/I Am is always aligned with and advocating for your highest and best. This energy is a powerful force of attraction that is always calling in the cooperative components required for that which you are desiring or asking for. It is the energy of joy, "all is well," *Conscious Neutrality*, unconditioned expression, and satisfaction. When you are in alignment and allowing, the feeling is one of expansion and all is well, versus always needing more or a needy energy. Needy energy, however it manifests, creates vibrational discord. Whenever you feel needy or negativity—when you feel the need to be sure that you are safe, to be taken care of by someone else, anxious, fearful, doubt-filled, etc.—know that you are out of alignment with your inner BEing!

When you push against anything, you create resistance, and that resistance lowers your energy and creates a new dominant vibration.

Your dominant vibration creates the point of attraction for the vibrational signal that you radiate. This signal is what goes forth to do its work in the unified field of consciousness and possibility.

You are always in relationship with your Source, but the type of relationship is up to you. You are the one who allows things to influence that relationship, to establish a fear or faith vibration. What type of vibration do you want to be the energetic influencer of your reality?

You cannot serve two masters; you must choose which one will be your dominant vibration!

Allowing a negative thought and feeling to be the dominant vibration of your being influences your vibration and deactivates the positive energy you had flowing. Yet you have free will: it is your choice! How can you quickly shift energy? Ask these quantum questions:

- Is this an influence (**master**) I want to perpetuate (**serve**)?
- Is this an experience I want to keep having?
- What active, dominant vibration do I want to experience now?
- What master vibration do I want to serve, Spirit or ___?

Do Not Worry, Take No Thought, and Seek First the Kingdom
MT. 6: 25 - 34

Seek first the kingdom. Be in alignment with a higher vibration, lift your eyes to a higher realm of awareness, a higher resonance in the multidimensional spectrum. Seek first the kingdom and consciously shift to something more interesting. Do that and THAT energy will respond in kind. It is the law!

Do not be anxious. Take no thought. Be not concerned with what is going on around you. Look at all things from an energetic perspective. This does not mean you do not think; it means that you ALLOW your thoughts to be oriented toward action to BE inspired by Spirit/Universal Presence. When you are in energetic alignment with higher vibration, that vibration goes before you to prepare the way, make straight the path, and to rearrange the matrix (an environment in something grows). You do not have to take any thought; the higher dimensional frequency does the work through you—It performs an alchemical transformation experience that occurs right before you.

Do Not Judge, Not Seeing Log in Your Eye While Seeing Speck in Another's, and Do Not Throw Pearls Before Swine
MT. 7: 1 – 6

Judge not, lest you be judged. Consistently learn to shift your energy to a higher vibration and awareness when things appear to be going awry or you do not like what you see. Stop giving meaning to things and stop being a made-up meaning-maker. You do not know the reason for everything.

Do not see the annoying speck in another's eye (energy field) until you have requested to see how you carry this same energy. We are mirrors for each other.

Do not throw pearls before swine. When you are engaging in a field of perceived incoherent energy—holding an energy of higher awareness and you sense it, see it, know it humbly, and yet others do not see it that way—shake off the energy and move on. Don't take it personally, don't try to change them, don't force an issue. There is nothing personal about it. It is an energetic dynamic of two different types or levels of energy fields colliding. It is not right or wrong. It is about readiness and being ripe for change and new levels of information. Do not waste energy trying to convert others to your way of knowing. If they are not ready, they cannot see it through the same lens that you do. Don't fight, resist, retaliate, or try to be right. Instead, shift your energy to higher levels of awareness. And remember, every time you try to convert someone to your way of thinking or feeling, you actually lower your vibration to meet theirs. Ponder this! Be the space of **A.L.L.O.W.** (**A**lways **L**et **L**ight **O**pen the **W**ay).

KEY ELEMENT ATTRACT — MT. 7:7-29

Attraction supports inspired action that is in vibrational alignment with who you BE!

Having aligned in this consciousness, your actions will be inspired by higher dimensional awareness and frequency and will attract alchemical transformation experiences, synchro-divine events, and the highest possibility in the unified field of consciousness.

Know that the higher the vibration you send forth consciously, the more impact it has on the field and the more you add to the overall consciousness of greater good for all as a collective whole. As you are alchemically transforming your life, you are imprinting a higher vibration onto the field and supporting the capacity for a new awareness in collective consciousness, regarding the establishment of spiritual principles in mind (abundance, etc.).

Ask and It Will Be Given, Golden Rule, The Gate is Narrow, Beware of False Prophets, By Their Fruits They Will Be Known, BE a Wise Builder, and When Jesus Finished the Crowds Were Astonished For, He Taught as One with Authority

Matthew 7: 7- 29

Ask and it will be given. The work of *Soul Mastery* and being a master facilitator of energy is to KNOW that in this state of receptivity, of alignment and allowing, you can *ask and it will be given*. And then the work is to relax while the attracting forces organize in the field of all possibility to bring to you the highest and best of that which you are aligned with.

To attract a big dream requires that you believe big. It requires, according to the law, that you create a big vibrational momentum of YES energy that has the capacity to catapult your ideas and possibilities into manifestation. This doesn't happen with a "yes, but!" That is why *the gate is narrow*!

Golden Rule. Do unto others as you would want done—regardless! Be the **Golden Rule** in action. Be willing to treat others as you want to be treated. This is expressing unconditioned love. Unconditioned love is different from third-dimensional conditioned love, as is currently being lived. Conditioned love means that you must act a certain way or I won't love you any more or respect you any longer. Conditioned love has perceptual boundaries holding it in place and you are happy as long the conditions are met. If and when they are not met, it makes you unhappy and you fight and argue for your perceptual limitations and boundaries to be reestablished.

The gate is narrow. The path is straight and narrow. Meaning that the higher the frequency, the less opportunity there is for wallowing in any type of negativity or show-stopper conversations. We're talking about the *yes, but; what if, if only, you don't understand, if only I was . . .* As your energy field rises in dimensional frequencies, manifestation becomes more instantaneous, therefore you must stay aware of what you are setting vibrationally into motion in every moment. Ask yourself the question over and over, "Is this vibration I am holding serving me?" A simple question whose impact is far reaching. As your energy rises, what can be held in the vibrational field of thought and feeling becomes subtler and subtler because what influences the energy must stay pristine and light. Appreciate, appreciate, appreciate! Blessing confers energy upon a thing. An 1800s metaphysician, Emma Curtis Hopkins, said, "Demonstration is rest." Once you have demonstrated a spiritual principle in consciousness, sit back and get ready . . . Do not worry about anything.

Wise builder. You are the ***wise builder***, selecting higher vibrational ground to build your foundation. Beware of those who tell you that you are Pollyannaish or that you just don't live in reality. Over time, they will see your life works. Build on solid spiritual principles not appearance.

By their fruits, they will be known . . . It is never "Why is this happening to me again?" You know why! Align with a higher energy and it will not happen again—or if it does, you won't care anymore because your perception has shifted. Perception has everything to do with how and what we will receive, so it is not about faking it 'til you make it! When you are faking something, what is the energy that underlies that thought? It is, "I am not this, but I will pretend."

Energy doesn't lie. It is better to find one thing you are good at and use that as your point of energetic appreciation than to try set up a field of fake-it-'til-you-make-it energy, for that sets up a subtle resistance because you know it is not true. So BE a field of energy. Appreciate one good thing about who you are and allow that to attract more possibility. *I am a point of great possibility in this grand universe.* Your words have power, so honestly be in appreciation and self-observation. Ask yourself, "Am I arguing for my limitations, or aligning to greater good through my words and actions?" Why would you ever want to talk about what you don't want, when you know and understand that law responds to you as a vibrational point of awareness and attraction? Stop arguing for your limitations in order to be third-dimensionally right or justified. You cannot help suffering if you are suffering; you cannot shift anger if you are angry; raise your vibration first, then you can be in service to others in accord with the level of vibration you are holding.

Every word uttered energizes the ethers with a creative VIBRATIONAL impulse that in due season brings forth its image and likeness...
Our bodies are weak or strong according to what we decreed for them...
in accord with the obedient life and substance...
The vitamins in thought are 1000 times more life giving.
Charles Fillmore, July 30, 1933

He taught as one having authority. Unconditioned love is a harmonic field of resonant energy and people recognize when they are in its presence. When you BE a field of harmonic resonance, you know your joy is not dependent on anyone else in order for you to stay in vibrational alignment, which means that another does not have to act a certain way for you to love them—or yourself.
When this field of harmonic resonance energy (unconditioned love) is established, it holds a wisdom and knowledge vibration that is beyond third-dimensional influences. Holding this energy field of unconditioned love, you know when to engage and when to leave.
In this consciousness, you recognize when a field you are entering is holding discordant energy and you make your decisions about what to do next from a higher wisdom and awareness. You do this without making the other person wrong or being in judgment about them. You just notice the field of energy and you BE interested in what you are noticing, without judgment or attachment. You notice and choose to make a choice as you are inspired or guided. And people recognize that your energy is different, that your energy inspires them.

Attraction holds action. Let it **BE** inspired action. An action that is always oriented toward the highest good of all, without greed or malice or "me first." Attraction supports inspired action and thus does NOT force outcomes. Inspired action invites the good of all to be paramount in the unfolding process. Inspired action does not manipulate people or situations, either for their own good or to increase personal good! This is often subtle and you must stay alert and aligned to perceive which energy you are calling forth. Mastery is about consciously aligning with, rather than manipulating, the law.

Who you **BE** vibrationally determines the level of inspired action you can attract and act from. Will you attract as ideas for action from the guidance of Higher Awareness/God/Inner Being/Source Energy/Spirit? Or will you attract from your own human-survival-oriented ego? Each produces a different result in the unified field of consciousness and impacts the level of possibility and potential available to you in the moment. **Attraction** supports inspired action in **align**ment with who you **BE**!

BE the knowledge, information, light, and understanding of the *Sermon on the Mount*. **Blessed are** you who **BE** these attitudes (aligned fields of energy) in action! For wherever you go, you confer a higher, lighter energy upon the fields in which you are interacting. For you now hold a dominant vibration that arises from a higher dimension of awareness, and energy doesn't lie!

Attract & Synchro-Divinity

When you **BE** in **alignment** and **allow**, you hold a state of awareness that is receptive to the multidimensional energies flowing without resistance and you discover that the time-space continuum collapses. The time-space continuum dissolves and the universal energies begin to work effortlessly on your behalf to attract the highest possibilities that you are aligned with in the unified field of consciousness; and synchro-divine events are now attracted to you, effortlessly. Synchro-divine events are those unexpected and yet seemingly miraculous events that begin to emerge within the field of your awareness. Synchro-divine events are often unbidden and uncalled for, yet they shift your reality as they unfold.

These synchro-divine events come, revealing themselves through people, situations, and conditions to bring to you what you need before you even had an idea that it was wanted. They come to reveal mini miracles—right doors opening, right people showing up, information shared that shifts the trajectory of your life in that moment, and more.

Attract & the Role of Appreciation

As you **BE** the energy of Conscious Neutrality in action, you carry the energy of knowing that this is a YES universe. You know that the Universal Impulse is always attracting more to you, in alignment to your state of receptivity. Your perception has everything to do with how and what you are receiving, for it creates the state of receptivity for who you **BE**!

Who you **BE**, also includes your cells. Every cell of your being has substance (divine energy), life (the perfect pattern of wholeness), and intelligence (an inherent wisdom that knows all things). Your cells hold emotional memories that support and attract to you based upon what you perceive is happening in the moment. Thus, they either support you as a field of creative energy or a field of resistant energy. Both appreciation and resistance play a part in cellular epigenetic regulation. Illness is believed to be the result of prolonged resistance held in your energy field, as it turns down the rheostat that governs and supports your cellular gene light of well-being. Appreciation turns it up and lets the good energy flow! Thus, appreciation is a powerful tool in the alignment and activation of the universal flow of energy.

Also, through your appreciation of all things, people, conditions, and situations in your life, you can appreciate yourself into transformation. Everything and everybody in your life is a portal of information — energetic forms of manifestation appearing — to show you what you want, or what you don't want to experience in your life. Therefore, appreciate all things appearing in your life, for the energetic messages they are giving you, about how you want to live your life. BE a wise builder, this is a YES universe and appreciation is a catalytic spark plug!

A&A: Social Action Through Conscious Neutrality

You can't see a new reality until you do the work to rent the illusionary veils that hold the information of that reality at bay. With this is mind, consider the possibility that the following scenario is a metaphysical treatise on the next phase of evolution of spiritual, social action. It is a template on how to energetically participate in spiritual social action from a *Soul Mastery* awareness.

As you begin this exercise, you are invited to put all pre-prescribed ideas and notions you hold about the man named Jesus aside. It doesn't really matter whether he lived or if he did or did not do all the things "they" say he did! What is important is that through the legacy of his story and life experiences, even if they are a myth, are woven mystical teachings that are discoverable by those who have *eyes to see*.

Jesus and the Woman Caught in Adultery
John 8:1-11 A *Woman Caught in Adultery*

> 1 Jesus returned to the Mount of Olives, 2 but early the next morning he was back again at the Temple. A crowd soon gathered, and he sat down and taught them. 3 As he was speaking, the teachers of religious law and the Pharisees brought a woman who had been caught in the act of adultery. They put her in front of the crowd. 4 *"Teacher,"* they said to Jesus, *"this woman was caught in the act of adultery. 5 The law of Moses says to stone her. What do you say?"* 6 They were trying to trap him into saying something they could use against him, but Jesus stooped down and wrote in the dust with his finger. 7 They kept demanding an answer, so he stood up again and said, *"All right, but let the one who has never sinned throw the first stone!"* 8 Then he stooped down again and wrote in the dust. 9 When the accusers heard this, they slipped away one by one, beginning with the oldest, until only Jesus was left in the middle of the crowd with the woman. 10 Then Jesus stood up again and said to the woman, *"Where are your accusers? Didn't even one of them condemn you?"* 11 *"No, Lord,"* she said. And Jesus said, *"Neither do I. Go and sin no more."* (New Living Translation)

With Jn. 8: 1-11 as the foundational context for your responses regarding spiritual, social action, ponder the following ideas:

- Consider this! Was the man named Jesus in this scenario taking a stand for spiritual social justice and action? If your answer is yes, ask yourself: Was Jesus taking that stance through resistance or a connection to the flow of inspired action [higher dimensional awareness]?
- Consider what influenced the outcome. Was Jesus perhaps in alignment with higher dimensional energies?
- Consider the possibility that Jesus saw no wrong, that he was a field of nonresistance, non-defensiveness, and power.
- Consider all this the next time you want to take a spiritual, social action. What is the consciousness from which you want to take that action? Fight thinking or right thinking?

~6~
Alignment Practices for Dissolving 3rd Dimensional Fear-Based Patterns

A. *Stimulus-Response Mechanism of Brain*
Academy of Coaching Excellence®. Maria Nemeth, Ph.D. (adapted)

You are a meaning-making machine. Without being consciously aware, you are continually creating **Conclusions** about your environment, welfare, safety, people, situations, conditions, and life. You create your **Conclusions**, from the results of experiences you have had, or from embedded perceptions and beliefs. Once you create a **Conclusion**, you give it great meaning. You believe, based on your **Conclusion**, that this is what is, and what will always be. If something comes up to create any doubt about the **Conclusion**, you will go forth and gather evidence to assure you are right regarding the meaning you gave it. Your experiences, then, will reflect this assurance back to you. "See, I told you I was right."

You (and the collective we) are wired for this — it is how the mind works! Your brain's Limbic System (Amygdala) is continuously scanning the environment to decide if there is safety and balance or separation and perceived threats. Your brain will stay in this stimulus/response mechanism until you shift your **Conclusion**, to something more interesting.

Stimulus/Response Mechanism of the Brain

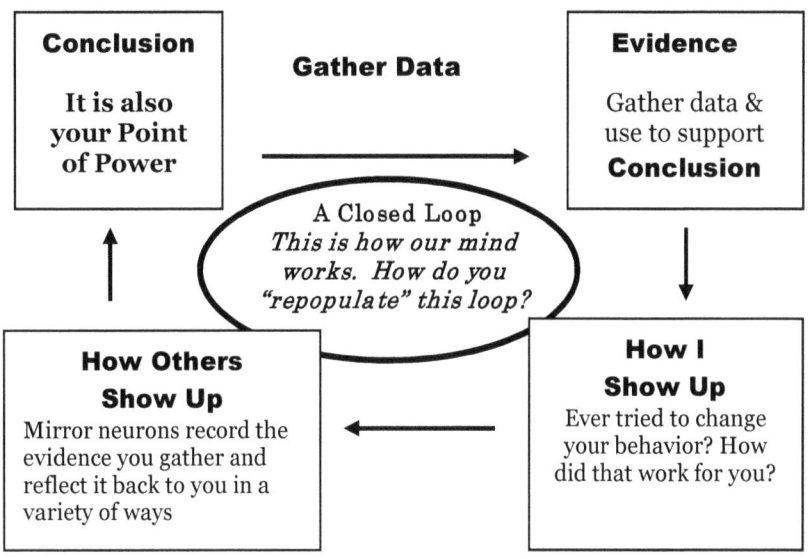

B. 3 Concentric Circles Model – Who Am I?

Carl Jung, Ph.D., Academy of Coaching Excellence ® Maria Nemeth, Ph.D. (adapted)

Circle 1 – Who I Pretend I Am
Who I am when I am in putting on my "face", in public, at a party, or meeting new people, it is my public pretense. It is not necessarily made up or make-believe, it just who I put forward, as a pretense. I act all bubbly when I meet someone, and excitedly greet them with a, "hi there," or I shrivel and shyly, say "hello."

Circle 2—Who I Am I Afraid I Am — My Sub-Personalities; My Persona, Mask, &/or My Shadow
Who I worry I am and what I fear is missing or broken in me and that others might see. So, I cover it with persona or mask as a protective-defense mechanism. Or, shadow behaviors I don't necessarily see, arise and run me. They each arise as a protective-defense mechanism.

Circle 3 – Who I Really Am – Authentic Self
The truth **IS** – I Am whole and complete! The Authentic Self, the Hero, **is** "who I really am" in the world. As Authentic Self, I know who I am, I know my core values, and what is important to me. When I demonstrate who I really am I experience coherence. When I am not demonstrating who I really am, my – **Authentic Self** – I demonstrate who I am afraid I am, or pretend I am (and I experience incoherence).

C. Authentic Self & Personas, Masks, & Shadows

Adapted from a work by Robert Assagioli, Ph.D.

**Sub-Personality Roles:
Persona's, Masks, & Shadow Aspects
Assumed as a protective front &/or defense mechanism**

Persona's, Masks, & Shadow aspects are sub-personality types that you assume, use, or take on as a protective-defense mechanism in order to: feel safe; to feel justified; to not be seen; to be seen as special; to assure you are not recognized; to not to live up to your potential; because you are afraid; etc. They include behaviors such as:

Sarcastic, cynical, withdrawal, self-deprivation, sour grapes, preaching to make your point, grudge holding, needing to be right, flooding someone w/information, victim, poor me, playing dumb/stupid, endless explanations, being too nice, acting crazy, no humor, taking offense, illness, confused, wanting to have last word, blaming others, high charge of energy in body, feeling explosive, inappropriate laugher, rigidity, counter attacks, denial, making fun of others, trivializing w/humor, other_____

Or, role identities you take on: mother, father, rich, poor, good girl, bad boy, sick child, care taker, daddy's girl, people pleaser, savior, martyr, etc., other_____

__Being as honest as possible, circle all of the above that you utilize.__

Instructions: After circling all that you use, select the 5 you use the most. 1. _____ 2. _____
3. _____ 4._____ 5._____

Identify the one that you use most! #1. _____
Answer the questions below — be as honest as possible!

Sub-Personality Roles, Persona, Masks, Shadows (P/M/S)

*The #1 default-protective-defense mechanism/role I assume is:
_____

*Give this role (sub-personality) a name! *Ms. Know-It-All*
_____

*The type of situations, conditions, or persons behaviors that trigger me into assuming this role (sub-personality) are: (this is not about right/wrong but being in self-observation)
_____
_____

*When I am in this role the behaviors I exhibit, assume, or communicate include:
_____
_____

*When I am wear my role what I am really afraid people will see is:
_____
_____

*When I am in this role I feel/my payoff is:
_____

*When I am in this role how I treat others is:
_____

The Authentic Self - Integrated Mind, Body, Soul

*Rename your P/M/S role into a more positive manner:
Ms. Know-It-All becomes **Holder of Wisdom**
_____

* Visualize yourself in this new identity!
* Let this new expression of you begin to take hold & speak for itself.

* Consider, what one action you can take or new behavior you can shift into — that is a more accountable action or practice — when you notice that you are wanting to, or beginning to, act from your P/M/S?
_____
_____

D. Universal Alignment Invocation as a Practice

The swift powerful activity of Universal Intelligence
now releases from me
all thoughts, beliefs, behaviors, ideas, and energies
that <u>are not</u> in vibrational alignment with
the universal principles of truth.

The swift powerful activity of Universal Intelligence
now attracts to me
all persons, thoughts, beliefs, behaviors, ideas, and energies
that <u>are</u> in vibrational alignment with the
universal principles of truth and the
highest possibilities in the unified field of consciousness.

Instructions:
Repeat a minimum of twice a day, once in the morning upon arising, and then again, before you go to bed. Do this for a period of no less than 21 days.

Please note that the word **person** is not listed in the first paragraph of the Invocation, this is deliberate. Do not add it! From a higher dimensional awareness, and metaphysical teaching perspective, you never request that a person be released from your life. Instead, you ask that you learn the lesson that the person is there to teach you, and to learn it quickly. For once the lesson is learned the person will leave, or you will be so transformed that their presence doesn't bother you any longer.

E. Micro-Meditation: An Embodiment Practice

A spiritual practice does not have to be an hour long to be effective. It is more about how you intentionally focus your attention and energy towards the practice, than the amount of time. In this, micro-meditation embodiment practice, you are intentionally focusing your attention and energy in the heart space, and then, on connecting with the energy that is "alive" and resides in the heart space. Energies such as, the spaciousness of emptiness, the Unified Field of Consciousness, and the crystalline Christ Energy (crystalline means, very clear).

This is both a practice for the development of *Soul Mastery,* and *Conscious Neutrality.* Remember, when you open yourself to the awareness that holds the state of BE-ing *Conscious Neutrality* in action, neutrality does not mean that you do not care. Neutrality is not about --not caring but about—not carrying. Not carrying any longer, lower vibrational energy, or negative emotional residue.

When you consciously connect with the Christ Energy/The Field for even a brief moment, you become one with that Field, you hold that energy, and people notice and experience that energy emanating from you. And when you BE this energy in action, this is the greatest act of Sacred Service you can perform. For you are an energy changer, in service to the greater good of all. It can be no other way, for this is what this Field of energy holds.

When you consciously surrender, over and over, into The Field of higher dimensional awareness, The Field/Spirit/Source begins to guide your actions, creates inspiration and inspired thoughts and actions, and these will all arise from a level beyond, reason and intellect, even illumined intellect.

Instructions:

First, create an intention. Intend to commit to this spiritual practice, until you know that you are consciously in alignment with The Field/Christ Consciousness. Hold also, a commitment to engage with the spiritual practice at least twice per day, or more, for a minimum of 7 days. (Remember, this is not about a long practice, it is the development of an intuitive sensing and embodiment practice.)

The first several times, as you engage the practice, it may take five or ten minutes, or longer. Then as you consciously connect with the Light Energy, over and over, it will become an automatic response mechanism that you consciously tap into, with your eyes open, in the moment of a heartbeat.

Personally, I find that is akin to the ancient *Prayer of the Heart,* practice. Where the pilgrim, seeking to know how to pray without ceasing, asked the wise one, "How often do I have to do this prayer? And the wise one replied, "a thousand times a day, until the Prayer, begins to pray you."

Micro-Meditation: An Embodiment Practice

Close your eyes.
Take a deep breath and follow the energy of the breath into the heart space. Imagine that as your breath reaches the heart, it lands in the midst of a ball of Golden Light.
It is the field of crystalline Christ Energy/the Unified Field of Higher Awareness, that resides within you, at all times.
Your breath is moving in the midst of this golden field of energy.
You are one with this field, this Crystalline Christ Energy, this Spaciousness of Emptiness - that is in Unity with All Things.
You are That!
Notice that the crystalline Light begins to expand, and your Essence, along with it.
The Light expands and expands — you are aware that it is filling your entire heart space.
Now it is expanding out further and filling your entire being.
The expansion continues, as it now expands beyond the artificial boundary of body — your true Essence is expanding — and as it is expanding it is affecting your cellular structure, and your DNA — Light is expanding out from them.
Gently, with every breath, imagine that you are pushing the Light out into the room. Fill the room. Then reach beyond the room.
Finally, out into infinity.
Expand, Expand, Expand the Light.
You are now in Unity with all things, and your presence and essence carry the Crystalline Christ - Golden Light Energy.
You are now, the energy of *Soul Mastery*, and *Conscious Neutrality*, in expression and action.
You BE the presence of all is well and, in your presence, alchemical transformation takes place — with ease and grace.
Ameyn, Amen, and it is so!

Lightning Source UK Ltd.
Milton Keynes UK
UKHW021422201020
371910UK00009B/2045